The Apostle
PETER

The Apostle
PETER

Outline Studies on His Life and Writings

by
W. H. Griffith Thomas

Foreword by
John F. Walvoord

Introduction by
Warren W. Wiersbe

KREGEL PUBLICATIONS
Grand Rapids, Michigan 49501

The Apostle Peter, by W. H. Griffith Thomas. © 1984 by Kregel Publications, a division of Kregel, Inc., P. O. Box 2607, Grand Rapids, MI 49501. All rights reserved.

Library of Congress Cataloging-in-Publication Data

Thomas, W. H. Griffith (William Henry Griffith),
  1861–1924.
  The Apostle Peter.

  Reprint. Originally published: Grand Rapids, Michigan:
Wm. B. Eerdmans Pub. Co., 1946.
  Bibliography.
  Includes index.
1. Peter, the Apostle, Saint. 2. Apostles–Biography.
3. Christian saints–Palestine–Biography.
4. Bible. N.T.–Biography. 5. Bible. N.T. Epistles of
Peter–Commentaries. I. Title.
BS2515.T47   1984   225.9'24[B]   84-1493

  ISBN   0-8254-3823-3 (pbk.)

2 3 4 5 6 7 Printing/Year 94 93 92 91 90 89

Printed in the United States of America

CONTENTS

PART 1—LIFE AND CHARACTER

6 / Contents

PART 2—THE EPISTLES

FOREWORD

THE enduring quality of biblical truth is seen in the fact that many books written by outstanding Christian scholars years ago are still as up-to-date in their content as they were when they were written, because they are based upon the timeless Word of God. Such is the case with the work of W.H. Griffith Thomas, *The Apostle Peter: Outline Studies in His Life, Character, and Writings*.

Dr. Griffith Thomas in his lifetime was a recognized scholar who, on the one hand, was thoroughly aware of the literature available in theological or biblical fields, and, on the other hand, had the capacity to interpret the Bible in non-technical terms. Such is the evaluation of his book on the Apostle Peter. While many books have been written on the Apostle Paul, Peter has not enjoyed the same extensive studies. This book helps to remedy this lack and is a work which will provide much insight into the noble character of the Apostle Peter.

The presentation of the contribution of *The Apostle Peter* falls into two major parts: the first deals with the life and character of Peter, and the second deals with the truth revealed in his epistles. Accordingly, the reader will find a comprehensive spiritual evaluation of the Apostle Peter, including a discussion of many aspects of his life and witness, and at the same time a fine exposition of 1 and 2 Peter, the two books that Peter contributed to the New Testament.

Because the Apostle Peter has been unduly exalted by the Roman Catholic Church, there has been a tendency in Protestantism to ignore his leadership of the Apostles. This book will provide a needed corrective and at the same time many inspirational and factual truths that can be derived from his life and writings.

The re-publication of this great work will undoubtedly help to perpetuate these important teachings for a new generation.

President   JOHN F. WALVOORD
Dallas Theological Seminary

INTRODUCTION TO THE AUTHOR

HIS advice to young preachers was, "Think yourself empty, read yourself full, write yourself clear, pray yourself keen—then enter the pulpit and let yourself go!"

William Henry Griffith Thomas (1861–1924) followed that counsel himself, and in so doing, he became one of the spiritual giants of his day. As a preacher and a teacher of preachers, he excelled in spiritual depth, practicality, and a simplicity of expression that made the most profound truths come alive with excitement.

His mother was widowed before he was born, and family financial demands forced him to leave school when he was fourteen. He was converted to Christ through the witness of some friends on March 23, 1878. The next year, he moved to London to work in an uncle's office.

But Griffith Thomas was determined to get an education, so from 10:30 P.M. until 2:30 A.M. each night, he gave himself to serious study. He became a lay curate in 1882, while attending lectures at King's College, London, and was ordained in 1885. Griffith Thomas belonged to that early fellowship in the Anglican Church that was unashamed to be called "evangelical."

The day he was ordained, Griffith Thomas was admonished by the Bishop of London, William Temple, not to neglect his Greek New Testament. The young minister took that word to heart and, for the rest of his life, read one chapter a day from the Greek New Testament! This kind of devotion to God's Word shows up in his writings.

He ministered at St. Aldate's, Oxford, and St. Paul's, Portman Square (London), and in 1905 was named principal of Wycliffe Hall, Oxford, the evangelical center for Anglicans studying for the ministry. He taught there for five years, then moved to Toronto to join the faculty of Wycliffe College, where he taught for nine years. He and his family then moved to Philadelphia and Griffith Thomas entered a wider ministry of writing and Bible conference work. He was associated with some of the leading preachers and conference speakers of his day and often spoke at large Bible conferences.

He joined with Lewis Sperry Chafer and others to found Dallas Theological Seminary and was to have taught there, but his death on June 2, 1924, interrupted those plans.

WARREN W. WIERSBE

Back the Bible Broadcast
Lincoln, Nebraska

PREFACE

THE main purpose of these Outline Studies is to offer Christian people some help and guidance in their personal meditation of the Scriptures, and, if it may be, some additional materials for closer study in view of Bible-class work. If the Outlines are worked through, Bible in hand, with a constant and careful use of the references given, it is hoped that further lines of thought and application will be suggested.

A short bibliography of the Life and Epistles of St. Peter is appended. All these works have been consulted or used in the preparation of these Studies; and while there is a general indebtedness to all, special mention must be made of one book to which my indebtedness is, I am thankful to say, very great. I refer to Bruce's *Training of the Twelve*,* one of the great books of the nineteenth century, and one which may be read with unhesitating confidence and unfailing delight and profit by all Christian people.

_____

*published by Kregel Publications.

Part 1
Life and Character

1

CONVERSION

BIOGRAPHY is very prominent in the New Testament, and is of great value for study. It enables us to see human nature as it is in itself, and to note what is becomes by Divine grace. Simon Peter's life is of particular interest. Personally, as a striking revelation of human character and Divine transformation; officially, and in relation to the Church, because of his prominent position. He is always named *first* (Matt. x. 2). He had a special and important sphere of labor (Gal. ii. 7).

A. HIS EARLY ASSOCIATIONS

1. **His name,** Simon (John i. 42). His father, John (John i. 42 and xxi. 15; Matt. xvi. 17, R.V.). His brother, Andrew (Mark i. 16; John i. 40). His wife and wife's mother are referred to (Mark i. 30; I Cor. ix. 5).

2. **His home influences.** He was probably brought up among those "who waited for the consolation of Israel" (see John i. 41, for expectation; cf. Luke ii. 25, 38, and xxiv. 21). Lived at Bethsaida, on the coast of Lake of Galilee, and by trade was a fisherman (John i. 44; Mark i. 16).

B. HIS EARLY CHARACTER

1. Impulsive.

2. Hot-tempered: drawing sword in Gethsemane (John xviii. 10).

3. Blend of courage and cowardice (Gal. ii. 12).

4. Bargainer: "What shall we have?" (Matt. xix. 27).

5. Boastful (Mark xiv. 29).

6. Self-confident (Luke xxii. 33; John xiii. 37).

7. Possibly swearer: oaths at the denial as recurrence of former habit (Mark xiv. 71).

N.B.—Yet many think these were not necessarily profane oaths, but solemn asseverations. In either case the fact of the guilt is the same (see *He Chose Twelve*. By Dr. Elder Cumming).

C. HIS CONVERSION

Study John i. 41 f., and note the stages.

1. **The preceding influences:**

(*a*) General: Messianic expectation.

(*b*) Special: Preaching of the Baptist.

2. **The human instrument:**

(*a*) His brother, Andrew.

(*b*) The two methods, testimony and influence. He *taught* and *brought*. Note here the two elements of Christian service, *preaching* and *persuasion*.

3. **The Divine power:**

(*a*) Penetration: "Jesus beheld."

(*b*) Perception: "He said, Thou art . . ." These impressed Simon with the Divine knowledge of Jesus.

4. **The Divine claim.** The new name given implied the claim of authority (cf. Old Testament changes of names, Abram and others). Somewhat similar to change of name at marriage; it meant a new position and new responsibilities.

5. **The Divine promise:** "Thou shalt be called 'Rock'" was a clear reminder at once of his need and of the assured supply. He needed firmness, strength, stability, and these elements should certainly be his ("Thou *shalt be* called,") and should come to him in contact with Christ and in discipleship.

Note the close and necessary connection between conversion and character. Christ at once linked Simon's initial coming with his subsequent experiences. Conversion is intended to lead to consecration, and therefore to character, without any *hiatus* or gap (Rom. xii. 1, 2).

6. **The immediate outcome.** Prompt acceptance by Simon of the new relation and the commencement of the life of discipleship.

CONCLUSION

1. **Note the Divine selection in Ps. lxv. 4,** and consider the four stages of every true life.

2. **Ponder the Divine action.** Here grace commences work on a soul, revealing the man to himself and the Saviour to the man.

3. **Consider the human response.** Trust and surrender. This is the one gateway to discipleship. Only a scholar at first, but all else comes.

4. **Dwell on the Human possibilities.** What grace can do as seen in Simon Peter. The process

was long and painful, but the result was certain. Note carefully all the usages of the names "Simon" and "Peter" in the New Testament. (1) The old name is occasionally seen after the new was given. Collect, study, and see force of the instances where "Simon" is used by our Lord. They are very significant and suggestive (see especially Matt. xvi. 17 and Luke xxii. 31). (2) But the new name gradually and surely makes its way. "Thou art *Peter*" (Matt. xvi. 18). "I tell thee, *Peter*" (Luke xxii. 34). "Go and tell . . . *Peter*" (Mark xvi. 7). (3) And after Pentecost there are only three instances of "Simon." The old had become transformed, hallowed, beautiful by the grace of God.

2

CALL TO MINISTRY

AFTER entrance upon discipleship come earliest lessons and impressions. After conversion (John i. 41f.) we find Simon Peter with Jesus at Cana (John ii. 1-11), and sharing in the impression of His "glory" through that first "sign." Probably also he was with Jesus through the Judæan tour (John ii. 12 and iv. 4) of eighteen months, or some part of it, gaining still deeper insight into the Master from personal contact. Here is a hint to young converts of the need of learning before teaching. Then, on return to Galilee (John iv. 43), Peter seems to have gone back to his ordinary work of fishing.

Now comes a SECOND STAGE, involving call from ordinary discipleship to special ministry (see Matt. iv. 18-22; Mark i. 16-20; Luke v. 1-11; and study the last-named in particular). Probably this miracle was used almost exclusively as an appropriate means of the calling of Peter and his fellow-fishermen. Consider, then, three stages of the call.

A. THE PREPARATION (LUKE 5:1-5)

1. **How appropriate the circumstances** (vv. 1-3). People pressing to hear the Word. Our Lord enters Peter's boat. "Put out a little"—for the purpose of preaching.

2. **Then comes the simple command:** "Put out into the deep" (see R.V.). "Let down your nets for a draught"—a test for Peter's faith and obedience.

3. **The significant response of Peter needs attention.** Are they the words of prompt faith, or are they expressive of doubt and hesitation? Probably the latter, as though he said, "Master, we toiled all the night, the best time for fishing, and took nothing; and now in the light and brightness of day a draught of fishes is surely unlikely. Yet I will let down the net, though I feel sure it will be useless." Jesus had said, "Let ye down [plural] your nets [plural]." Peter responded with, "I will [singular] let down the net [singular]," just to show the result would be fruitless. (N. B.—The text of the A.V. is followed here, as inherently more probable.) So the answer was possibly (*we* would say, in view of sequel, *certainly*) an answer, not of prompt and reverent faith, but of reluctant and partial obedience. This was so like Peter.

B. THE PROGRESS (5:6-9)

1. **Unexpected success** was the immediate result.

2. **Great surprise** was naturally evinced by the fishermen. The quantity of fish at such an unusual time, at the order of One Who was not a fisherman, and Who, presumably, knew nothing about fish and fishing! A reminder of His Divine power over nature and of His Divine knowledge.

3. **Realized** sinfulness is soon definitely expressed by Simon Peter, who cries: "I am a sinful man, O Lord." Why? **What made him feel his sin** at this juncture? What connection was there between the miraculous draught and this confession of **sin**? On another occasion of a miraculous draught he did not realize his sin, but, instead, hurried to meet his Master, and that soon after the sin of his denial (John xxi. 7). Was it not that he now realized the sin of his own distrust which prompted the answer about toiling all night? Had he let down the *nets* of both boats, they would probably not have been broken. It is as though it flashed on Peter that, after all, His Master knew more about fishing than he did. His Master's knowledge and power were evident, and now the disciple rises to a higher conception of the One before him. He had called Him "Master" (v. 5), he now calls Him "Lord" (v. 8). Peter at once gains a higher idea of his Master and a *lower idea* of himself—both results very necessary for the ministry. The Lord reveals Himself to Peter, and reveals Peter to himself, to make him a greater blessing to others in the future.

C. THE PURPOSE (5:10-11)

1. **Notice the loving assurance given** (v. 10). "Fear not." How sweetly it fell on the heart of the awestruck disciple!

2. **Mark the higher work promised** (v. 10). "From henceforth thou shalt be continually catching men" (Greek).

3. **See the full consecration shown** (v. 11).
"They left all and followed Him" (cf. Matthew's
and Mark's accounts). The old life, the old work,
the old associations were left for new life and service. Now these humble fishermen are known the
world over as Apostles of Christ.

The above interpretation, though not the usual
one, seems to harmonize best all the conditions
of the situation. Peter's impulsiveness in telling
his Master what he thought, and his condor in
confessing his error and sin, are thoroughly
characteristic.

SUGGESTIONS FOR MEDITATION

1. **The Master's purpose revealed.** A call upward and onward. From discipleship to service.
New trials and tasks are to develop character,
and prepare for more and higher work.

2. **The Master's plan stated.** He came to Peter
while engaged in the ordinary work of life, and
used his boat for preaching, and the work of fishing to illustrate and prepare for the higher service. So God tests us in and by ordinary daily
life, "the daily round, the common task," to lead
to higher things. What a responsibility this puts
on common life! It is easy to be a Christian under
exceptional circumstances, but it is difficult to
glorify God in daily life by faithfulness and
obedience. God is ever coming to us in simple and
ordinary ways. "Faithful in that which is least"
(Luke xvi. 10).

3. **The Master's purpose endangered.** It might
have been frustrated by Peter's hesitation. He
began to reason, and nearly missed a blessing,

and did actually miss some blessing by only a partial obedience. We often miss blessing by not doing at once what we are told. The possibilities of blessing are endless if we obey, while partial obedience necessarily forfeits blessing.

4. **The Master's plan accepted.** Peter was recalled and brought back to a right state of mind; he accepts Christ's plan loyally; he obeys, and is blessed. "Faithful response to heavenly teaching is a sure precursor of heavenly grace." "Whatsoever He saith unto you, do it' (John ii. 5).

5. **The Master's purpose realized.** The fisherman responded to his Master, and is led on to higher and nobler work. He becomes a "fisher of men." How appropriate as a symbol was his old work as a fisherman! What are some of the qualities of a fisherman that are also needed by "fishers of men"?

(1) **Watchfulness.** Ever alert (Heb. xiii. 17; Ezek. iii. 17 and xxxiii. 2-7; Acts xx. 26-28).

(2) **Patience** (2 Tim. ii. 24). Impatience in Christian work causes the soul of the worker to suffer.

(3) **Persistence** (2 Tim. iv. 2). Activity, energy, and keeping "always at it."

(4) **Courage** (2 Tim. iv. 5). Sea fishing involves taking one's own life in one's hands.

(5) **Tactfulness** (2 Tim. ii. 24, 25). Wisdom to win (Prov. xi. 30). A worker who is "winsome" will surely "win some."

(6) **Self-forgetfulness** (1 Cor. xv. 10). Fishermen must keep themselves out of sight.

3

EARLY LESSONS

AFTER the call to definite ministry (Luke v. 1-11), involving constant and close association with Jesus, we have to consider the special training of Peter leading up to, and immediately following, his choice as one of the Twelve. It is necessary to study every passage very carefully, and to try to realize the particular impression made on him by our Lord, and what special aspect of Peter's character is revealed. We must bear in mind the continuous influence of our Lord on Peter by reason of *continuous* fellowship, even though now we study only those incidents where Peter is particularly referred to, and observe only some of the results of the training.

A. A SERIES OF EVENTS

1. **The healing of Simon's wife's mother** (Matt. viii. 14f.; Mark i. 29-31; Luke iv. 38f.). Suggestive as to his domestic life and personal associations. Peter was a married man (I Cor. ix. 5). (Is it not curious that Rome should have singled him out as their founder, seeing that they insist on celibacy for priests?) Evidently the disciples already had confidence in Jesus as a healer, for at once "they

tell him of her." Note the homely side of His ministry. A Saviour for the individual, for the needy, for the home.

2. **Our Lord's popularity** (Mark i. 36-39 and ii. 1-12). Note in i. 36, *"Simon and they* that were with him." Clearly he was already a leader among them. Leaders will always come to the front. Our Lord's popularity manifestly impressed His disciples (i. 37), and His reply, so deliberately avoiding popularity, must have surprised them.

3. **The choice of the Twelve** (Matt. x. 2-4; Mark iii. 13-19; Luke vi. 12-19). A landmark in the history. The third stage in Peter's history: (*a*) Discipleship (John i. 41f.); (*b*) Ministry (Luke v. 1-11); (*c*) Apostleship (Luke vi. 12-19). Hitherto our Lord had been working almost alone; but the work was increasing, and division of labor became necessary. He thereupon organized a band, and sent them forth. Of the Twelve, eleven from Galilee, only one (Judas Iscariot) from Judaea. Four were fishermen. At least two pairs of brothers were included, and at least one pair of friends. The names are recorded in four lists (Three Gospels and Acts i.). Peter's always comes first, and Judas's always last. Why was Peter put first? Possibly the force of personal character which fitted him to lead disciples and early Church. Our Lord's choice was made after a night of prayer (Luke vi. 13), for it was evidently an event of deepest importance. In Mark iii. 14 we see the twofold purpose of the appointment, "that they might be with Him" (fellow-

ship), "and that He might send them forth" (service). The second depends on the first. Contact with Christ qualifies us for work for Him. Keep this order and preserve due proportion. We must "abide" in order to work. Work is the proof and expression of fellowship. The work was twofold (Mark iii. 14, 15), preaching and healing, words and deeds.

4. **The woman healed** (Luke viii. 45). Again Peter is the spokesman. "Somebody hath touched Me." What an impression of the clear perception of their Master! A great lesson for Peter.

5. **The raising of Jairus' daughter** (Mark v. 37; Luke viii. 51). Only "Peter and James and John" went in. Why these and not Andrew? Probably these were men of exceptional power, and so in need of exceptional training. Certainly they became the three most prominent of the original Twelve. Another display of their Master's power. A beautiful combination of tenderness and strength: "Talitha cumi"—"My little lamb, arise" (so in Aramaic). The second occasion of raising the dead (Luke vii. 11-16), though some think Jairus' daughter comes first.

All these and other events went to make up the "Training of the Twelve" and of Peter in particular. Consider now—

B. A SUMMARY OF EXPERIENCES

1. The disclosures of the Master

(*a*) His power over sickness, sorrow, and even death.

(*b*) His sympathy. Human needs ever touched Him. Distinguish sympathy (feeling *with*) and pity (feeling *for*). Sympathy is only possible when we put ourselves in the other's place.

(*c*) His humility. Imagine Peter's delight at the crowds following his Master. "All men seek Thee" (Mark i. 37). How surprised Peter must have been at the Lord's avoidance of popularity! Caroline Fry's definition of humility is "unconscious self-forgetfulness." See how and whence Peter learned the lesson (I Pet. v. 5, 6).

(*d*) His knowledge. Peter was constantly being made aware that he was in the presence of One Whose knowledge was deep, full, far-reaching, Divine (*e.g.* our Lord's knowledge of the woman's touch).

2. The impressions on the disciple

(*a*) The need of help. So much sorrow, suffering, need, death. Here was a constant call to sympathy and help. Eyes open to see men's need of the Gospel, and hearts longing to give them the blessing, are two necessary marks of true discipleship.

(*b*) The value of earnestness. How deeply must Peter have been struck with our Lord's strenuous life! (Mark i. 39-45).

(*c*) The duty of work. The "choice" men in Old Testament and New Testament were always hard workers, always chosen for special service. Abraham, Moses, David, Daniel, Paul, would have had an *easier* life if they had not been called of God to special work. "Many are called, but few are *choice*." The "choice" men always "toil terribly."

(*d*) The deepening of trust. This is the profoundest impression made on Peter. He must have been growing in trust at every step. This is ever the chief lesson to learn. The way to learn it is to live in the presence of Christ. The better we know Him the more we trust Him. Peter grew in faith as he lived with Christ. "Faith cometh by" the direct revelation of Christ to the soul as we study His Word and abide in Him. In proportion to our fellowship will be our faith and then our faithfulness (Rom. x. 17).

4

DEEPENING IMPRESSIONS

THE revelations of the Master to the disciple, and the impressions of the Master on the disciple, were necessarily continuous and ever-deepening; but this constant influence was accentuated from time to time by specially important lessons. Such were the Walking on the Sea, the Feeding of the Five Thousand with the incidents arising out of it, and the Discourse on Eating with Unwashen Hands.

A. A LESSON ON FAITH (Matthew 14:19-33)

Peter's most constant and pressing need was a deepening trust in his Master. This was only possible in proportion as the Master revealed Himself in fresh aspects of His character. Study the Walking on the Sea from this standpoint.

1. **A new revelation.** "Among the ancient Egyptians the symbol of impossibility was the simple figure of two feet planted upon a fragment of ocean." The disciples had been in difficulty, "toiling in rowing." Jesus comes to them and does what was humanly and physically impossible—walks on the waves. A revelation of Divine power in a new, startling, and suggestive form.

2. **A characteristic response.** Imediately on hearing the voice and receiving the assurance, "It

is I!" Peter replied: "If it be Thou, bid me come." Note the "If." Jesus had said, "It *is* I." How characteristic this mingling of doubt ("if") and faith ("bid me come")! What prompted the request? Mere impulse, or personal vanity? Desire to do something unusual and extraordinary? Probably a mixture of rashness and conceit. His rashness was a rebound from his former despair after physical exhaustion to hope on seeing Christ.

3. **A sharp reminder.** Now Peter is to learn his lesson. Jesus only said, "Come," as if permitting rather than (as Peter wished) "bidding." He was just allowed to have his own way. So he starts, and for a while all is well. But soon comes the test. The state of wind and waves led to fear. Then his faith at once went, and he began to sink. But the Master was near, and in an instant Peter was safe, not, however, without a rebuke about his lack of faith. Peter had already been reminded of his own sin (Luke v. 8); now he was reminded of his own weakness.

(1) Faith is evoked by the personal revelation of the Master to the soul (v. 27).

(2) Faith is expressed by the soul's appeal to the Master (v. 28).

(3) Faith is exercised by the soul's response to the Master (v. 29).

(4) Faith is weakened by the soul putting circumstances between it and the Master (v. 30).

(5) Faith is renewed by the merciful interposition of the Master (v. 30).

(6) Faith is instructed by the loving rebuke of the Master (v. 31).

(7) Faith is deepened by the new revelation of the Master (v. 33).

B. A LESSON ON EXPERIENCE
(John 6:66-71)

1. **The great sign** (John vi. 1-15). The only miracle recorded by all evangelists. A turning-point in Christ's life. It led to the attempt to make Him King (vi. 14, 15), and this in turn to the testing and sifting consequent on the discourse in Capernaum.

2. **The great messages** (vv. 22-65). Note the stages carefully marked:

(a) vv. 22-40, Discussion.

(b) vv. 41-51, Dissatisfaction.

(c) vv. 52-59, Dissension.

(d) vv. 60-66, Defection.

Then comes as the crowning result—

(e) vv. 67-71, Devotion.

3. **The great conviction**

(a) The testing of the Twelve. "You will not go away, will you?" (Greek. Jesus anticipates a *negative* answer.

(b) The answer of Peter. (1) Where else? "To whom?" (2) What they enjoyed: "Thou hast." (3) What they felt: "Thou art."

(c) The terrible revelation. One of the Twelve a "demon" (vv. 70, 71).

(1) Experience of Christ leads to the consciousness of awful alternatives. "To whom?"

(2) Experience of Christ is realized in the forms of *truth* and *life*. *"Words . . . life."*

(3) Experience of Christ is gradual in stages (believe and know), but with permanent results (both verbs are in the perfect tense). "We have believed (and are still believing), and have come to know (and are still experiencing)."

(4) Experience of Christ is based on His personal character and His relation to God. "The Holy One of God" (R.V.).

C. A LESSON ON KNOWLEDGE
(Matthew 15:15-20; Mark 7:17-23)

1. **Religious formalism** (Mark vii. 1-9). Note the circumstances and our Lord's rebuke. Mark the three stages of formalism: v. 8, leaving God's word for man's; rejecting God's word for man's; v. 13, making void God's word by man's.

2. **Ignorance** (Matt. xv. 15f.). Peter could not understand this exalted standpoint, and asks for an explanation. Our Lord is surprised that at this stage ("ye also even yet") he should be unable to appreciate it. Old ideas die hard. Discipleship does not easily throw off old customs and associations. It is only as we continue in Christ's Word that we are "disciples indeed," "come to know the truth," and "are made free" (John viii. 32-36).

3. **Spirituality** (Matt. xv. 17-20; Mark vii. 19). Our Lord shows whence true spirituality comes and wherein it consists. Not bodily foods, not ceremonial and p h y s i c a l cleansings; but thoughts, desires, determinations, constitute

the essence of spiritual life. Note R.V. of Mark vii. 19; "This He said, making all meats clean." Does this put an end to the Jewish distinctions of clean and unclean? If so, it has a bearing on Acts x. 15.

(1) Spiritual knowledge comes from close adherence and loyal obedience to the Word of God (Mark vii. 6-13).

(2) Spiritual knowledge distinguishes between ceremonialism and the soul's true relation to God (Matt. xv. 10-14).

(3) Spiritual knowledge realizes that life works from centre to circumference, and not *vice versa* (Matt. xv. 15-20).

CONCLUSION

1. Consider the necessity of these three lessons

(*a*) Without faith it is impossible to be a true disciple.

(*b*) Without experience it is impossible to be a strong disciple.

(*c*) Without knowledge it is impossible to be a clear disciple.

2. Consider the order of these three lessons

(*a*) Faith leads to experience.

(*b*) Experience leads to knowledge.

(*c*) Faith, experience, and knowledge lead to power and blessing. See this order clearly in Rom. xv. 13, 14; I John ii. 12-14.

5

THE GREAT CONFESSION

AFTER a period of school life comes the examination. The daily influence of Master on disciple is now to be tested and the results revealed. A turning-point in Simon Peter's history, a landmark in his experience. Study Matt. xvi. 13-20; Mark viii. 27-30; Luke ix. 18-21; and note carefully the precise stages.

A. THE GENERAL INQUIRY
(Matthew 16:13-20)

1. **Where made?** In North Palestine. When in retirement ("He was praying alone," Luke ix. 18).

2. **Why made?** Several opinions were now rife about Him. But these were not definite or true enough, and so another step was now to be taken.

B. THE PERSONAL TEST (16:15)

1. **Its Novelty.** Hitherto our Lord had revealed nothing about Himself. Such a disclosure would have been premature. It was far wiser to leave His character and influence to make their own silent but deep impression.

2. **Its meaning.** A new stage upward. His earliest word was, "Follow Me!" implying trust

and obedience. Now it is, "What think ye of Me?" *Conviction* is thus shown to be necessary as well as *confidence*. *Ideas* are of primary importance to full discipleship. Ideas and convictions about Christ are the natural and necessary outcome of contact with and confidence in Him. "Love with all thy *mind*" (Luke x. 27) is an integral part of our relation to God.

C. THE DEFINITE CONFESSION (16:16)

1. **Of our Lord's Messiahship.** "The Christ."
2. **Of our Lord's Divinity.** "The Son of a living God."

(N.B.—Compare this with the earlier and shorter confession in John vi. 69, R.V.: "The Holy One of God." Mark the progress of conviction: (1) Character, "Holy One"; (2) Office, "The Christ"; (3) Authority, "Son . . . God."

D. THE SPECIAL COMMENDATION (16:17)

1. **Its nature.** "Blessed art Thou." Blessedness in *confessing* and also in *possessing*.
2. **Its secret.** "For flesh," etc. Spiritual discernment was the explanation of this. The daily contact and gradual influence had done their work, and now had come an unusual inflow of knowledge on his experience.

E. THE GREAT COMMISSION (16:18-19)

1. **The promises** (v. 18). A difficult passage, evidently arising directly out of Peter's confession.

It is our Lord's acknowledgment of that and of what it involved.

(*a*) Study carefully the terms used: "Thou art *Petros*," "and on this rock" (Greek, *Petra*.. See R.V. *marg.*). "My Church," "the gates of Hades."

(*b*) What is the meaning of "this rock"?

(1) *Is it Peter himself?* If so, how? Note, "Thou *art* Peter" (cf. John i. 42, "Thou *shalt* be called Peter"). Now the change had come: "art" for "shalt be"; and as thus changed he should, by his life and work, be the instrumental foundation of the Church of Christ. His spiritual life is to be the basis of his fitness. Personal qualification is to issue in personal work.

N.B.—This view makes no distinction between *Petros* (masc.) and *Petra* (fem.), which, it is urged, would not be made in the Aramaic our Lord spoke. It is certainly a natural view, and is held by many modern scholars, among them Dr. Hort, whose great learning, together with his strong disagreement with Romanism, gives the greatest weight to his opinion (see his *Christian Ecclesia,* p. 17). It limits the meaning to Peter himself, and safeguards it against any Roman Catholic interpretation.

(2) *Is it Peter's confession?* This view takes "this rock" to mean "this confession of My Messiahship and Divinity you have now made"—an interpretation which agrees with I Cor. iii. 11; Eph. ii. 20; I Pet. ii. 4-8. The last passage is a very strong argument for this view, which also has the manifest advantage of distinguishing between *Petros* and *Petra,* as the Greek assuredly does. If our Lord meant

Peter himself it would have been most natural to have said, "And on thee will I build."

For a union of these two views see the valuable work by Principal T. M. Lindsay on *The Church and Ministry*: "The rock on which the Church was to be built was a *man confessing,* not the man apart from his confession, as Romanists insist, nor the confession apart from the man, as Protestants urge" (p. 6).

(*c*) "My Church." This is the first time of use of this word "Church" by our Lord. Note, too, the future, "I will build"; therefore, not then begun (until Pentecost).

(*d*) "Hades." The unseen world, the world of the spirits departed this life. "Shall not prevail," *i.e.* shall not keep back or retain any of Christ's followers. The usual interpretation of "gates of Hades shall not prevail," as indicating the futility of all active opposition to the Church, while true as a fact, seems scarcely possible as an explanation of the text. *Gates do not fight.* They open and shut, and our Lord here promises that not one of His followers shall be kept back from Him by the power of the grave (cf. Rev. i. 18, "I have the keys of . . . Hades").

2. **The duties** (v. 19)

(*a*) Study the terms used.

(1) "Keys." Symbol of authority (see Isa. xxii. 22; Luke vi. 52; Rev. i. 18 and xx. 1).

(2) "Kingdom of Heaven." Distinguish from "Church" (v. 18). Larger and wider idea. The Church is *in* the Kingdom. The Kingdom is the heavenly reign of God over all things earthly.

(3) "Whatsoever" (neuter gender); not "whomsoever." The reference is to *things,* not to persons.

(4) "Bind," "loose," are a Jewish formula for "prohibiting and permitting," and, taken with "whatsoever," imply disciplinary authority in the Church.

(*b*) Consider the meaning of the authority.

(1) It is personal. It doubtless refers to Peter's position in the early Church. He opened the Kingdom to the Jews (Acts ii.) and to Gentiles (Acts x.). He exercised disciplinary authority in the case of Ananias and Sapphira (Acts v.), and of Simon Magus (Acts viii.). Yet this authority to exercise discipline was not unique, for in Matt. xviii. 18 we find it given to all the Apostles. Peter's leadership, however, was undoubted, though the difference between him and the others was one of degree, not of kind.

(2) It cannot be continuous, *i.e.* beyond Peter himself, as Rome alleges. There is no authority for transmission, and no proof of it, because there is no possibility of it. It was obviously intended for him alone. Nor do we find any supreme authority exercised over the rest of the Twelve (see Acts xi. 2, where Peter was called to account for his action; also Acts viii. 14, where we read, *"They sent* unto them Peter").

To sum up:

The commission was a personal recognition of a personal confession, and was a promise and prophecy of special personal work in days to come.

SUGGESTIONS

1. **The value of a true creed.** It *does* matter what a man believes. Creed influences life. The finest creed is seen here: personal belief in Christ.

2. **The secret of a true creed.** How did Peter arrive at his belief? By personal contact with Christ. Conviction arose out of an experience taught by God.

3. **The confession of a true creed.** An absolute necessity for real life (Rom. x. 9; Matt. x. 32). And always brings blessing ("Blessed," v. 17).

4. **The connection between creed, confession, and service.** Cause and effect. What we possess we profess, and what we profess we propagate.

6

THE GREAT TEST

AFTER great blessing comes severe discipline. The
testing came to Peter through deeper teaching, new
and strange revelations of the Master, teaching
about the Cross. Until now there had been no
definite or clear word about the Cross. Nearly two
years of the ministry had passed without this revelation (see Matt. iv. 17, "From that time"; and Matt.
xvi. 21, "From that time"). It was disclosed in the
last year of ministry. All the earlier allusions had
been only vague, veiled, and indirect (see John ii.
19 and iii. 14; Matt. ix. 15; John vi. 51; Matt. xvi.
4). Now He spake "openly" (Mark viii. 32). Circumstances called for it. Storms threatened; the
end was approaching; above all, the disciples were
more spiritually prepared for it after Peter's confession. Study Matt. xvi. 21-28; Mark viii. 31-38;
Luke ix. 22-27.

A. THE MASTER'S REVELATION
(Matthew 16:21)

1. **Note the detailed statement.** A fivefold
revelation of the Cross.
   (*a*) Place—Jerusalem.
   (*b*) Experience—"suffer."

(*c*) Source—Jewish authorities.

(*d*) Extent—death.

(*e*) Outcome—resurrection.

2. **Consider the wise purpose.** The hostility of the Jews was rapidly coming to a head. There was no possibility of winning them. Hence the disciples must face the future; also their ambitions as to earthly Messiahship and glory must be checked and their ardour for temporal power and authority damped. Above all, they needed a reminder of the great facts of sin and redemption.

B. THE DISCIPLE'S RESPONSE (16:22)

1. **Consider his prompt action:** "Then Peter took Him," *i.e.* laid hold of His hand. Doubtless elated by the Master's glowing words (vv. 17-19) and in danger of pride; yet it was truly well meant and generous in intention.

2. **Remark his astonishing words.** Actually began to "rebuke" his Master, and said, "Pity Thyself [Greek]; this shall never be unto Thee," *i.e.* "Put pain and sorrow out of Thy life." "Sacrifice duty to comfort." Just as at the Temptation (Luke iv. 1-13), the suggestion was a "short cut" to the throne by avoiding the Cross. The very idea of suffering and death was intolerable to Peter.

C. THE MASTER'S REBUKE (16:23)

1. **Dwell on the terrible epithet:** "Satan." Only a little while ago "Blessed"; now, "Satan." An

awful contrast, and the one epithet was as real as the other.

2. **Ponder the sad explanation:** "Thou savourest not," etc. (R.V. "mindest"). The word implies the *whole* bent of moral being—mind, heart, and will (cf. the same Greek word in Rom. viii. 5, 6, 27; Col. iii. 2; Rom. xii. 16; Phil. iii. 19).

N.B.—May we not infer from Peter's silence that this rebuke was beautifully taken? At any rate, later on he had learned the lesson (see I Pet. ii. 20).

D. THE MASTER'S REMINDER (16:24-27)

1. **The new call.** "Then," *i.e.* arising immediately out of circumstances. Not only a cross for the Master (v. 21), but for the disciples also (v. 24). There great laws of discipleship: Denial of self; taking up Cross; following Christ. What is self-denial? Denial of *self;* not merely denying certain things to self, but denying *self,* abjuring self, doing to self what Peter did to Christ—*denying* it, ignoring it. "Not I." "None of self." What is "taking up the Cross"? We must never mistake our sins for the Cross. Bad temper, sloth, iritability, are not crosses, but *sins.* Our cross is God's will in daily life, even though (and especially *when*) it crosses our will. What is the meaning of to "follow"? Trust, imitate, obey.

2. **The threefold reason.** Note "for" in vv. 25-27.

(*a*) "For" (v. 25). It is the only true life.

(*b*) "For" (v. 26). There is nothing comparable with it.

(*c*) "For" (v. 27). The future will reveal its glory.

N.B.—Review the last study and this together in Matt. xvi. 13-28, and note—
(1) Christ Himself (vv. 13-17).
(2) Church of Christ (vv. 18-20).
(3) Cross of Christ (vv. 21-23).
(4) Confession of Christ (vv. 24-26).
(5) Coming of Christ (vv. 27-28). The whole Gospel is here.

LESSONS

1. **Our Lord's constant endeavour** (v. 21). It is to lead His disciples farther and deeper. "Lead me in Thy truth" (Ps. xxv. 5). He has "many things to say" (John xvi. 12).

2. **Our own deplorable contrasts** (cf. vv. 17 and 23). The hour of praise is the hour of peril. "A full cup is hard to carry without spilling." "A way to hell from the gates of heaven" (BUNYAN).

3. **Our Lord's faithful dealings** (vv. 23-24). There was no lowering of the standard to suit Peter's ideas. So now there is no reduction of His demand on us. He tells Peter *frankly* his sin and error, and repeats the demand with clearness. "Every man is the stronger for knowing the worst he can know against himself, and for acting on that knowledge."

4. **Our own perpetual need.** It is the Cross. The Lord knew this, and hence the emphasis. Notice, in Church history and individuals life today, these two great facts—

(*a*) Christian theology is always defective without the Cross.

(*b*) Christian experience is equally defective apart from the Cross (Gal. vi. 14).

Thus was Peter tested and trained. The best training for usefulness is the training of our own character in relation to God.

7

THE TRANSFIGURATION

THE revelation of the Cross at Cæsarea Philippi (Matt. xvi. 21) was a great mystery to the disciples. The Transfiguration occurred soon afterwards, and had a distinct bearing on this conversation of Christ and His disciples. The Transfiguration was a landmark in our Lord's history and in the history of the disciples. "It stands midway between the Incarnation and the Ascension, and it is the justification of our faith in the one and the warrant of our faith in the other." Consider it now with special reference to Simon Peter. Note again the three men taken. They had need of special training. Probably also they were more receptive than the rest.

Study Matt. xvi. 28 to xvii. 9; Mark ix. 1-10; Luke ix. 27-36.

A. THE TRANSFIGURED LORD

There was evidently a clear connection with the reference to "six days" and "about eight days."

1. **The time.** Note in all three Gospels the preceding conversation about the Cross. This is a key to the true meaning of the Transfiguration.

2. **The character.** It occurred to our Lord "as He was praying" (Luke ix. 28, 29). The Trans-

figuration was thus the direct result of communion with and communication from God. It affected both His appearance and raiment. It was the glorification of His humanity by His Divinity.

3. **The purpose.** What did it mean? It was clearly intended for the *disciples,* to remind them of the glory of their Master, in spite of the dreaded revelation of the Cross. Probably it was also to prepare them for the Cross—to show that His Divinity and His death were not irreconcilable; to prove that there was no contradiction, but a beautiful consistency between them. But had it also a purpose for *Jesus Himself?* May it not have been another assurance from the Father as the Son went forward to the Cross? Galilee had rejected Him; Jerusalem was soon to follow suit. In between comes this foretaste of the glory to follow.

B. THE ATTENDANT SAINTS

1. **Who they were.** Moses and Elijah. The great lawgiver and the great prophet. Representatives of the Old Covenant. Characteristic and special men. Also both remarkable as to their exit from the world (Deut. xxxiv. 6; Jude 9; 2 Kings ii. 11).

2. **What they said.** They spoke of His "decease" (Greek, *exodus*) at Jerusalem (Luke ix. 31). The very topic from which the disciples had been shrinking! The death of Christ was thus actually a subject of interest and conversation to inhabitants of the heavenly world. What a revelation to Peter!

The Law and the Prophets conferring as to his Master's death! That death would be the "end of the Law" and the fulfilment of prophecy.

3. **Why they came.** Doubtless as a further confirmation to the disciples of the need of the Cross. A reminder that there must be some deep reason for a transaction which occupied the attention of heaven. Again, probably these representatives of the Old Covenant were allowed to come for our Lord's own sake also, to strengthen Him in the fulfilment of God's will which had been anticipated and foretold by the Old Testament. It was the homage of the Law and the Prophets to the Divine Messiah.

C. THE ASTONISHED DISCIPLES

1. **Consider the three selected.** Why these? Probably to benefit all through the fittest. Others might have been dazzled, and Judas in particular incited to ambition. Perhaps even these three were only saved by keeping the event secret. We can see the unfitness of the nine by the incident at the foot of the hill (Luke ix. 37-42). God's revelation is possible only to fitted ones.

2. **Notice their slumber.** Is not this almost inexplicable under the circumstances? Their Master's glory and all the attendant incidents could not keep them awake. Their spiritual condition was evidently none too strong and real, even though by comparison it was better than that of the rest of the disciples.

3. **Study their words.** On being thoroughly roused, Peter was again the spokesman. Mark very carefully what he says: "It is good for us to be here." The words are often quoted as the expression of a rapt experience, as the realization of great privilege and adoring gratitude for the honor. But the original Greek will not bear this interpretation. *Literally,* "it is good [or beautiful, or fortunate, or excellent] that we are here." There is no "for us," as of personal advantage, in the Greek, and the word for "good" does not mean precious or valuable, but "outwardly attractive," excellent, opportune. Peter's meaning is, "Master, it is opportune that we are here, to be of service to Thee. Let us make three tents." He thought the Kingdom had come (see Luke ix. 27), and that places of sojourn were needed. How like Peter! Always the well-meaning blunderer!

N.B.—Clearly this is the true view, for we are told that he was "sore afraid" (Mark ix. 6), and that he "knew not what he said" (Luke ix. 33), which would not be correct if the words expressed his own delighted experience.

D. THE DIVINE TESTIMONY

1. **The cloud.** It came as the direct result of Peter's words (Matt. xvii. 5; Luke ix. 34). God's will about Moses and Elijah staying was at once shown when Peter suggested the tents. Now Moses and Elijah are hidden.

2. **The voice.** "This is My beloved Son." Such is the Divine testimony. The other two are only

servants. "This is My Son," and He must not be put on a level with the others by the erection of three tabernacles. The hour had come for the departure of the Law and the Prophets. As Jews, probably Peter and the other two were glad that Jesus was, after all, connected with Old Testament saints. So the reminder came (cf. Isa. xlii. 1; Heb. i. 1, 2).

3. **The command.** "Hear Him." For the future He is to be the whole object of attention, trust, and obedience. "Hear Him," especially when He speaks of the Cross, and do not shrink from it.

E. THE PRACTICAL RESULT

1. **The full reassurance.** After their fear came "Fear not" and their Master's "touch" (Matt. xvii. 7). In the comfort of this they soon recovered, and "Jesus only" was full of meaning to them.

2. **The immediate impressions.** These were not very deep or strong, as is seen from their discussion going down the hill (Matt. xvii. 10-13).

3. **The permanent recollection.** It was only after Pentecost that they recalled this glorious event and its meaning. As to John, see John i. 14; and as to Peter, 2 Pet. i. 16-18. Peter never forgot that night, nor its revelation of the glory of his Master.

SUGGESTIONS

1. **God's meaning in the Transfiguration**

(*a*) To bear witness to the glory of His Son. He is far above the Law and the Prophets, and is the unique and final exponent of the Divine will.

(*b*) To emphasize the glory of the Cross. **This** is the fitting topic of heavenly interest and the supreme object of His Son's Incarnation.

(*c*) To create permanent impressions in the disciples about His Son and the Cross. Truths already received are to be made real in experience. Creed must be transfused into life. New views are to develop new vitality.

2. God's method in the Transfiguration

(*a*) Bringing and leaving disciples face to face with His Son: "Jesus only."

(*b*) Concentrating attention on His revelation: "Hear Him."

(*c*) Occupying the mind with the Cross as central, and showing its entire compatibility with, and appropriateness to, the glory of the Son of God.

8

A LESSON ON HUMILITY

FROM the Mount of Transfiguration to the valley of duty. After high communion and new teaching comes daily living. Our Lord's "Training of the Twelve" is henceforth concerned either with the Cross or with the true spirit and character of His followers. Lessons on humility are specially prominent. Study carefully Matt. xvii. 24-27 (R.V.).

A. THE TAX

1. **What it was.** See R.V. and study Exod. xxx. 11-16; Exod. xxxviii. 25-28; Neh. x. 32. The tax was religious, not civil; Jewish, not Roman. It was the regular tribute to the Temple worship.

2. **What it implied.** The acknowledgment of God's claim, the duty of God's people to uphold their sanctuary. In our Lord's case the contrast between the Transfiguration and taxation is striking and suggestive. It was indeed a call to humility in a definite shape and concrete form.

B. THE TAX-GATHERER AND PETER

1. **The tax-gatherer's question:**

(a) Was it sincere? It may have been asked in strict official duty and with proper courtesy. Rabbis were known to claim exemption as teachers. Did Jesus make the same claim?

(*b*) Or was it to entangle? If the payment were admitted, how could He claim to be "greater than the Temple"? (Matt. xii. 6). If declined, how could He be a true Jew and not support the Temple?

2. Peter's answer

(*a*) Its motive was good. It was prompted by zeal for his Master's honor, as though to say, "Of course He pays the Temple tax. He will not be behind others in legal and loyal action."

(*b*) Yet its unwisdom is evident. It failed to remember and recognize his Master's true position as "Son of God" after the Transfiguration (Luke ix. 35) and what was involved in it (see below on v. 25).

C. THE MASTER AND THE DISCIPLE

1. The conversation

(*a*) Our Lord took the initiative (v. 25) in order to teach Peter a special and needed lesson. It was not an argument against paying the tax so much as a reminder about right meaning and motive.

(*b*) Our Lord's question needs careful consideration. The point of it is that kings do not demand taxes from their own *children,* but from their *subjects* (a prince, as a boy, would not be expected to pay taxes to his father, the king).

N.B.—There is no reference here at all to Jews (sons) and Gentiles (strangers). This point does not enter. Peter's reply shows that he understood what his Master meant. "From strangers," *i.e.* those outside the family circle. "Then are the sons excempt." Mark the significant claim here made by Jesus, to be occupying a unique relation to God as compared with other Jews. He is the Son; they are the subjects.

2. The command

(*a*) "Go . . . and take . . . and *give*." Note the "Me and thee." How beautifully the Master associates Himself with His disciples, and yet distinguishes between Himself and them!—"Me and thee," not "us" (cf. John xx. 17).

(*b*) "Lest we cause them to stumble." "Peter had committed his Master, but his Master would not commit Peter." Liberty was asserted and yet set aside.

THE MEANING

1. **Our Lord's genuine humiliation.** He fulfils every requirement of earthly law to its last detail (see Matt. iii. 15). He thought equality with God not a prize "to be retained" if He could by humiliation win men (Phil. ii. 6, R.V.). What was a tax of half a shekel (15d.) in this connection.

2. **Our Lord's supreme claim.** Yet in His humility there is majesty. He deliberately distinguishes Himself from the Jews. Though He is a Jew by birth, He is uniquely "Son of God." Study His claims as they are more fully and frequently stated in St. John's Gospel.

3. **Our Lord's unerring wisdom.** He will not be, or put, a stumbling-block (Luke vii. 23). His humility prevents Him from *taking* offence by Peter's too ready answer to the collector. His love

prevents Him from *giving* offence by withholding the tax. Let not your good be evil spoken of" (Rom. xiv. 16). "Woe . . . because of stumbling-blocks" (Matt. xviii. 7).

4. **Our Lord's perfect knowledge.** He knew where the fish was, what was in the mouth, and that it would meet the need exactly; half a shekel for each.

5. **Our Lord's wonderful power**. All nature at His command. Time, place, circumstances, all arranged. Bengel calls attention to six points in this miracle. (1) Something was caught. (2) Caught quickly. (3) Money in a *fish*. (4) in a fish's *mouth,* and so easily available. (5) Just what was needed. (6) A Roman silver coin, and so current.

N.B.—This was the only miracle worked for our Lord's own benefit. Can we not imagine the profound impression made on Peter? "What a Master we have!" "What a marvel He is!"

9

A LESSON ON FORGIVENESS

IMMEDIATELY following the lesson on Humility comes one on Forgiveness. Study Matt. xviii. 21-35. Note carefully the deep underlying connection between humility and forgiveness (Bruce, *Training of the Twelve*).* Pride and vindictiveness go together. Personal ambition is usually very sensitive to injuries, quick to take offence, slow to forgive.

A. PETER'S QUESTION

1. **How it arose** (see v. 15). "Thy brother." Probably he asked for guidance in the practical application of our Lord's counsel (vv. 15-17); or possibly it may have been due to resentment consequent on the tax-gatherer's question (xvii. 24), which seemed to reflect on his Master.

2. **What it showed**

(*a*) Was it prompted by any suppressed feelings of resentment? Consider the previous dispute about "greatness" (xviii. 1-4) and the new teaching about the Cross (so foreign to Peter's prevalent ideas). The recent journeys of Christ and His Apostles had been in private in North Palestine. Peter preferred

---

*A.B. Bruce. *Training of the Twelve*. Kregel Publications. 1971.

popularity and crowds, and his feelings may have been hurt by the question about the tax.

(*b*) Or was it not rather a genuine desire to learn the Master's will on this matter? The Jewish custom was to bear injuries *three* times, and then to regard their duty as done. Peter wanted light on the subject. Note the mixture of his childlikeness and childishness: childlike in the earnestness and sincerity which would go up to seven times; childish in the thought that a repetition so many times and no more would be magnanimous. Note the precise form of the question, "My brother." Sad that *brothers* should do thus! "Sin against me." But may it not also be that I sin against him?

B. OUR LORD'S REPLY

1. **The meaning** (v. 22). Seventy times seven meant unlimited forgiveness (cf. Hebrew of Isa. lv. 7, "He will multiply to pardon"). This is God's method of forgiveness, what has been well called the "celestial arithmetic" of forgiveness. How surprised Peter must have been by this difference between seven and four hundred and ninety times! How puny and poor was his own love!

2. **The illustration** (vv. 23-34). Note three contrasts in the parable.

(*a*) The debts £2,000,000 and £4).

(*b*) The creditors.

(*c*) The doom.

3. **The application** (v. 35).

(*a*) The reason of forgiveness: "His brother."

(*b*) The thoroughness of forgiveness: "From your hearts."

(*c*) The certainty of retribution: "So also."

(*d*) The universality of retribution: "Every one."

C. FORGIVENESS IN THE NEW TESTAMENT

1. Its prominence

(*a*) In our Lord's ministry (Matt. v. 23, 24, 39-48, and vi. 12-15; Mark xi. 25; Luke xvii. 3, 4).

(*b*) In the early Church (Rom. xii. 14, 17, 19; Eph. iv. 32; Col. iii. 13; Phil. 18; 1 Pet. iii. 9).

2. Its necessity.
Study the Lord's Prayer. It is one condition of blessing being realized by us. Unforgiving spirit and harboring of grudges is fatal to spirituality.

3. Its meaning.
Three words are used in the Greek.

(*a*) Negative— *aphièmi,* to let go, remit; *apoluô,* to dismiss, send away, *i.e.* to remove the trouble.

(*b*) Positive—*charizomai,* to act *graciously, i.e.* to show a positively Christlike loving spirit, and not merely to *ignore* the past wrong. In Hebrew there are also three words for forgiveness: (1) to cover; (2) to lift off; (3) to send away.

4. Its secret
(Eph. iv. 23; Col. ii. 13 and iii. 13). The realization of what God has forgiven us is the only way of maintaining a forgiving spirit to others. "Keep yourselves in the love of God" (Jude 21).

10

A LESSON ON TRUE SERVICE

AGAIN we shall see how personal character and fitness were strongly emphasized by our Lord for His disciples. Now we follow the Master as He teaches Simon Peter what service really means. Study Matt. xix. 27-30 and xx. 1-16; Mark x. 28-31; Luke xviii. 28-30.

A. THE DISCIPLE'S QUESTION
(Matthew 19:27)

1. **Its occasion.** "Then." Study the context. It arose directly out of the rich young ruler's refusal to "leave all and follow."

2. **Its spirit.** "What shall we have?" Boast and brag. Contrast Peter's feelings with those of the rest (v. 25). They were afraid and astonished. He was complacent and self-satisfied.

B. THE MASTER'S REPLY (19:28-30)

1. **The encouragement** (vv. 28, 29)

(*a*) The reward of honor (v. 28). Note the disproportion. They 'left their *fishing.*" They should "sit on *thrones.*" Their "all" was comparatively little, but it *was* their "all," and so the Master honored it. Might not the very magnitude of the honor tend to keep them low? Compare the honor in which they are regarded now as the human and instrumental founders of the Church.

(*b*) The reward of requital (v. 29). Note the form of the promise—"thrones." Was not this an idea perilously near their worldly conceptions of Messiahship? Why did He not correct these ideas, instead of apparently confirming them? It has been suggested that He did it to allure them to higher ideas through the lower; that it was not delusion, but illusion. They would find the reality by-and-by. He does not always break our idols. He transforms them.

N.B.—Cf. Mark x. 30, "Now in this present time" and "with persecutions." Persecutions are actually regarded, not as drawbacks, but as part of the gain. In what sense does the Christian receive "a hundredfold *now*"? Clearly, not literally (hundred wives, children, etc.), but hundredfold of that which gives these things their value, the satisfaction they afford. Our capacity to enjoy increases. "*In* keeping *of* them [not *for* keeping them] there is great reward" (Ps. xix. 11). We may also compare Peter in the eyes of the world today. Has he not received his hundredfold in fame and praise and gratitude.

2. The warning (v. 30)

(*a*) The last first.

(*b*) The first last. Rewards are not determined by the *fact* or *duration* or *quality* of service, but by the *motive*. The right spirit in everything. Motive makes the man. Quality depends on motive.

C. THE MASTER'S ILLUSTRATION
(Matthew 20:1-16)

1. The parable explained (vv. 1-15)

(*a*) Note the key phrases: "agreed." This shows the justice of the Master. "What is right," *i.e.* the righteousness of the Master. "My will" (R.V.); *i.e.* being just to all, He may surely be generous to some if He wishes. Circumstances may vary, and some may have fewer opportunities. Are they therefore to suffer? "Eye evil"; *i.e.* envious of others' blessings.

(*b*) Compare and study carefully the three parables which deal with rewards. (1) According to *quantity* of work, *i.e.* when the ability is equal. "Talents" (Matt. xxv. 14-30). (2) According to the *ability* of worker, *i.e.* when the ability varies. "Pounds" (Luke xix. 12-27). (3) According to the *motive* of the worker. Laborers (Matt. xx. 1-16).

2. The parable applied (v. 16).

(*a*) "Many." Note the proportion. How sad! Why is it? Due to spasmodic and intermittent work. Not habitual faithfulness. "Few are *choice*" is a good interpretation or comment by way of application.

(*b*) Yet *not all*. "There are first who shall *not* be last." There are last who shall *not* be first. "Shall not the Judge of all the earth do *right?*" (Gen. xviii. 25).

SUGGESTIONS

1. The rewards of the Kingdom

(*a*) In the present. In Christ we find everything that makes kinship, relationship, property, possessions, attainments of the truest, highest possible worth. Also we find higher relationships and possessions, even spiritual and eternal. And in Him the possession and enjoyment of everything in grace, nature, art, science is deeper, richer, fuller. "All things are yours" (1 Cor. iii. 21).

(*b*) In the future. The crown and culmination of this life. God's purposes are not fulfilled here and now. They stretch over to the world to come.

2. **The risks of the Kingdom.**

(a) Because of the wrong spirit in the worker, and because of unfaithfulness in work.

(b) Resulting in absence of reward, loss of blessing, "saved [only] so as by fire" (1 Cor. iii. 15).

11

LESSONS ON JUDGMENT

As the crisis in our Lord's ministry approached, the lessons to the disciples became more and more solemn and impressive. During the early days of the week before the crucifixion the great future came especially into view, and also as part of it the destiny of the Jewish nation. Judgment was therefore prominent in our Lord's teaching, and two incidents in which Peter was concerned must now be considered.

A. JUDGMENT SYMBOLIZED
(Matthew 21:18-22; Mark 11:12-14,20-22)

1. The natural inquiry (vv. 18, 19)

(*a*) Our Lord's hunger. Literally, this was an illustration of His perfect humanity. Parabolically, it was a symbol of His seeking fruit in men's lives. God needs us and wants us. "Thou hast made us *for Thyself." "For Thy pleasure* they are and were created" (Rev. iv. 11).

(*b*) Our Lord's desire. Spiritually, it illustrated God's joy in man. God expects fruit in our lives; appropriate fruit, "after His kind" (Gen. i. 11); proportionate fruit; timely fruit.

2. The unexpected discovery (v. 19)

(*a*) Appearance of fruit, but not the reality. Abundant profession, but perfect destitution.

N.B.—Leaves attracted this attention because the time for figs (July) was not yet (it was April then); and the nature of the Eastern fig is such that *as soon as leaves come, figs should be there also.* Therefore He looked for proper accompaniment of the leaves.

(*b*) Reality being so different from appearance, our Lord bestows on it His malediction.

3. The solemn judgment (v. 19)

(*a*) Pronounced: "Let there be . . ."

(*b*) Effected: "Immediately . . . withered."

Symbolic action; exposition in *act* of a great truth otherwise taught in *words.* His judgment was not on barrenness, but on premature leafage without corresponding fruitage. *Hollow appearance of fruitfulness* was condemned; not barrenness, but hollowness, hypocrisy. Apply this to the Jewish nation then. How true! Apply to the lives of the Twelve. What peril!

4. The disciples' surprise (v. 20)

(*a*) Its cause. They were only surprised at the incident, as a manifestation of their Master's power. The *fact* only, not the *meaning.*

(*b*) Its suggestion. Their superficiality. They should have marvelled at the *law* and seen the *truth* intended. Just like people's astonishment at eloquence without any impression of the truth spoken.

5. The Master's lessons (vv. 21, 22). Jesus lifted the incident up again into the higher sphere, and makes it the occasion for two great lessons on

(*a*) The power of faith (v. 21).

(*b*) The prayer of faith (v. 22 and vv. 24-26).

B. JUDGMENT PROPHESIED
(Mark 13)

Soon came another opportunity for fresh teaching on judgment with special reference to the Jews. Simon Peter is again prominent.

1. The Master's revelation (vv. 1, 2)

2. The disciples' questions (vv. 3, 4)

(*a*) When?

(*b*) What sign?

3. The Master's answers (vv. 5-37)

(*a*) The danger of error (vv. 5-7, 21-23).

(*b*) The signs of the end (vv. 8-20, 24-32).

(*c*) The call to watchfulness (vv. 33-37).

N.B.—The above outline is necessarily brief, and intended only as a guide to the meaning of the Master's reply to the four disciples' questions.

1. Our one great need. Faithfulness.

The lesson of the fig-tree is against inconsistency, hypocrisy, unreality in religion; against profession without practice. It rebukes confession without conduct, and is against mere outward show in religion and what is only too well known as "cant." An affectation of saintlessness without the actuality is the most terrible thing in the world. Creed and conduct should be exactly balanced.

2. **Our one great loss.** Fruitlessness.

Why loss? Because fruitlessness means a permanent inability to help others. Fruit is intended for blessing and usefulness; and a fruitless Christian is not only not a help, but a positive hindrance.

3. **Our one great secret.** Faith.

(*a*) Faith links us to God and gives life.

(*b*) Faith clings to God and ensures reality.

(*c*) Faith receives from God and produces fruitfulness.

12

HUMILITY AND OBEDIENCE

THE day before the Crucifixion was particularly full of deep lessons for Peter. He with John had been sent to prepare the Passover (Luke xxii. 8); and now we turn to the consideration of the solemn teaching of the Upper Room so far as it concerned Peter directly. The first lessons are found in John xiii. 1-17.

A. THE MASTER'S REVELATION (John 13:1-5)

1. **His marvellous tenderness** (vv. 1, 2)

(*a*) To the last forgetful of self (v. 1).

(*b*) Even though all did not love Him (v. 2).

2. **His wonderful condescension** (vv. 3-5)

(*a*) At the moment of high consciousness (v. 3). Conscious of: (1) Sovereign power, "had given all things. . ." (2) Divine position, "came forth from God. . ." (3) Glorious prospect, "back to God." Yet He humbled Himself.

(*b*) In the form of menial service (vv. 4, 5) (cf. 1 Sam. xxv. 41). Query, Is it possible that He did this because *they* would not? (see Luke xxii. 24-27 for the possible explanation).

B. THE DISCIPLE'S RESPONSE (13:6)

1. **The astonishment.** "Thou" . . . "My."
2. **The motive.** Peter thought it derogatory to his Master's position and dignity.

C. THE MASTER'S REPLY (13:7)

1. **The statement:** "Thou knowest not now."
2. **The promise:** "Thou shalt know hereafter."

N.B.—"Hereafter" is explained by verse 12. Our use of it in reference to future vision as contrasted with present dimness is of course only an application. The "hereafter" to Peter was in a few minutes.

D. THE DISCIPLE'S REJOINDER (13:8)

1. **The vehement assertion.** Intended as devotion.
2. **The underlying spirit.** Really showing disobedience.

E. THE MASTER'S REBUKE (13:8)

Note our Lord's change of tone and words.
1. **The one condition:** "If I wash thee not."
2. **The awful possibility:** "No part."

So that the serious question for Peter was whether he was to be in Christ's Kingdom or not. Obedience is the secret of discipleship. Peter's first remark (v. 6) was really inconsistent with Christ's dignity, for if He had not humbled Himself there would have been no salvation. Peter's second remark (v. 8) was really subversive of Christ's Lordship, for if He does not wash us we have no part in the salvation He brings. In both instances Peter's own judgment is asserted, and thus real, though incipient, disobedience is shown. If Jesus is to be Saviour He must be Lord. Peter learnt the lesson later (cf. 2 Pet. i. 11, ii. 20, iii. 2, and iii. 18 for suggestive combination. See also Heb. v. 9: "Author of eternal salvation to them that *obey* Him").

F. THE DISCIPLE'S REQUEST (13:9)

1. **The great contrast.** "Lord, not my . . ." Peter's changes and contrasts are very noticeable. Note his mixture of good and evil and his swift change of moods. There is danger of feelings leading us astray. His heart's intent was right, but his judgment and spirit were wrong.

2. **The genuine fear.** Lest he should be outside after all. "If 'part with Thee' so depends, then wash all of me, not only my feet." Here was the other extreme. Overplus is, in a way, as bad as defect.

G. THE MASTER'S REMINDER (13:10,11)

1. **The right position** (v. 10).

(*a*) Justification is complete and permanent: "He that hath been bathed."

(*b*) Sanctification is progressive and continuous. "To wash his feet." Peter was already a disciple. His standing was secured and assured, but he needed the daily cleansing from defilement.

2. **The sad exception** (vv. 10, 11). Not all of them were clean. One was far from it (v. 11).

H. THE MASTER'S REASON (13:12-17)

Now comes the explanation (v. 7).

1. **The great claim** (vv. 12-14). He claims to be their "Lord and Teacher." Note in v. 13 "Teacher and Lord," the order of their *experience* of Him. But in v. 14 "Lord and Teacher." This is His standpoint. He is Teacher *because* He is Lord.

2. **The great duty** (v. 14): "Ye ought."

3. **The great example** (vv. 15, 16): "I," "Ye also."

4. **The great result** (v. 17): "Knowing," "doing," "happy."

SUGGESTIONS

"Washing the saints' feet" (I Tim. v. 10) is an important part of the spiritual duty of every believer, and these three rules for doing it have been aptly given. They deserve our careful attention.

1. **The water must not be too hot** (see Gal. vi. 1; 2 Thess. iii. 15; 2 Tim. ii. 24f.).

2. **The hands of the washer must be clean** (see Titus ii. 7; Titus iii. 2; 1 Tim. iv. 12).

3. **The washer must be willing to allow his own feet to be washed** (see Eph. iv. 32 and v. 21; Phil. ii. 3; 1 Pet. v. 5; Rom. xii. 10; and v. 16).

13

THE SOLEMN WARNING

THE hours spent in the Upper Room were fraught
with deep meaning to Peter, and were filled with
lessons which, when illuminated later by the Holy
Spirit, became prominent factors in his experience.
We now take up our Lord's announcement to His
disciple of the forthcoming denial. Study Matt.
xxvi. 31-35; Mark xiv. 27-31; Luke xxii. 31-34;
John xiii. 36-38).

A. THE DISCIPLE'S ANXIOUS QUESTION
(John 13:36)

1. **Its reason** (cf. vv. 33f.). The Master had
just announced His departure.

2. **Its motive.** Peter was evidently alarmed in
view of the separation and possible danger;
hence the abrupt question, which really implied,
"I will go also."

B. THE MASTER'S MYSTERIOUS ANSWER
(13:36)

Note how the actual question is ignored and the
unspoken thought dealt with.

1. **The present impossibility:** "Thou canst not." A moral one.

2. **The future certainty.** "Afterwards," *i.e.* when spiritually fit.

C. THE DISCIPLE'S PAINED SURPRISE
(13:37)

1. **The astonishment:** "Why cannot I?" He thought he was competent, and this was a reflection on him.

2. **The readiness:** "I will lay down my life." "If danger is all, I will die for Thee." Chivalrous, affectionate, sincere. Yet over-confident. He had soon forgotten the foot-washing.

D. THE MASTER'S SOLEMN REVELATION
(Luke 22:31,32)

Former lessons on self-confidence forgotten. This, however, is to make a lasting impression later on.

1. **The sifting** (v. 31). "You." In the Greek, plural, referring to *all* the disciples. Compare the sifting in John vi. 66. *That* was a sifting of false and true followers. *This* is a sifting of the false and true in His disciples.

2. **The protection:** "For *thee*" (singular), *i.e.* because of the greater need. Evidently a case of weakness rather than wickedness, though weakness is always *essentially* wicked.

3. **The outcome:** "When . . . strengthen." He is to help others by his own experience.

E. THE DISCIPLE'S RENEWED ASSURANCE (Luke 22:33)

1. **The boast of readiness.** Itself a fall.
2. **The ignorance of self.** Not even for prison was he ready.

F. THE MASTER'S PLAIN ANNOUNCEMENT (Mark 14:30)

1. **The denial clearly foretold**
2. **The details definitely stated**

G. THE DISCIPLE'S STRONG PROTESTATION (Mark 14:31)

1. **The last solemn avowal**
2. **The persistent ignorance of self**

SUGGESTIONS

1. **The disciple revealed**

(*a*) Utter ignorance of himself.
(*b*) Complete confidence in himself.

Self-confidence is always a mark of spiritual weakness and immaturity. Consider the awful possibilities of which we may be entirely ignorant. "Who can understand his errors?" (Ps. xix. 12).

> Beware of Peter's word,
> Nor confidently say,
> 'I never will deny Thee, Lord,'
> But, 'Grant I never may.'

2. **The Master revealed**

(*a*) Unerring knowledge: (1) Of us. (2) Of the foe. (3) Of our real needs.

(*b*) Unfailing love. (1) Warning. (2) Encouraging. (3) Assuring.

Hence (1) a true knowledge of self is only possible through a true knowledge of Christ. "In Thy light shall we see light" (Ps. xxxvi. 9). *Self*-examination is really impossible. We cannot fathom or understand the depth of our own heart. God must examine us (Ps. cxxxix. 23). *Self*-examination with a view to holiness is not really Scriptural. Holiness is only possible as we look away from self and are occupied with Christ. "Beholding . . . the glory of the Lord, we are changed into the same image" (2 Cor. iii. 18). (2) This knowledge of Christ is only possible through constant fellowship. We "know" in proportion as we "abide."

14

IN THE GARDEN

From the Upper Room we pass to Gethsemane, and notice how the disciples behaved after all the wonderful teaching and influence of those hallowed hours. It will be necessary to study Simon Peter:

(*a*) **During the agony** (Matt. xxvi. 37, 40, 45; Mark xiv. 33, 37, 41).

(*b*) **At the arrest** (John xviii. 10f.; Luke xxii. 50f.; Mark xiv. 47; Matt. xxvi. 51-54).

(*c*) **After the arrest** (Matt. xxvi. 56; Mark xiv. 50).

A. THE MASTER'S GREAT DESIRE
(Matthew 26:36)

1. **The need of prayer.** In the time of sorrow this was the refuge.

2. **The longing for sympathy.** In the moment of loneliness this was a strength. Note our Master's true humanity here. Prayer and sympathy are the upward and outward attitudes of the soul.

B. THE MASTER'S LOVING TRUST (26:37)

1. **Its reason.** The three selected were choice men of the Twelve. They had been so selected before.

2. **Its meaning.** For His own comfort and strength; also for their further training.

C. THE DISCIPLE'S SAD FAILURE (26:40)

1. **Its causes.** Physical fatigue and mental sorrow in view of their Master's revelations were the two causes of this sleep.

2. **Its revelation.** It showed spiritual incapacity. Even ordinary faithfulness was lacking, to say nothing of Peter's recent protestations of fidelity.

D. THE MASTER'S SORROWFUL SURPRISE (26:40)

1. **In the light of His own work** (v. 40). Three years of personal contact and spiritual influence. *"Could* ye not?"

2. **In view of Peter's bold assertions** (Mark xiv. 37). "Simon, sleepest *thou?"* As though to say, "After all that you have protested!"

E. THE MASTER'S SEARCHING LESSONS

1. **The call to readiness** (Mark 14:38). "Watch and pray." Spiritual alertness and spiritual dependence. These are needed especially because of the weakness of the flesh.

2. **The value of opportunity:** "Sleep on now." The time for helping Him is past. Opportunity never comes in *quite* the same way again.

F. THE DISCIPLE'S IMPULSIVE DEVOTION (John 18:10)

1. **The true intention.** He was no coward. He meant to show this after Christ's warning (cf.

Luke xxii. 35-38). Was not this very dull? As if *two* swords could suffice for *twelve* men!

2. **The great mistake.** He was really reckless. As if one man could do anything! He did not understand that circumstances needed not this method of defence. Possibly there was also a lurking pride and a desire to show his own courage.

G. THE MASTER'S SOLEMN REMINDER (John 18:11) (Matthew 26:53)

1. **The rebuke and its reason** (John xviii. 11). Resistance fails. What *could* he do?

2. **The uselessness and its reason** (Matt. xxvi. 53). Resistance is unnecessary. What *need* he do?

H. THE DISCIPLE'S UTTER DEFECTION (Matthew 25:56)

1. **The Master forsaken.** "They all," notwithstanding their solemn assurances.

2. **The disciple afraid.** Peter's own arrest was possible.

FAILURE

1. **Its characteristics**
(*a*) Failure of faith.
(*b*) Of love.
(*c*) Of courage.
The spirit was weak as well as the flesh.

2. **Its causes.** Dr. Bruce (*Training of the Twelve*) makes these suggestions:
(*a*) Lack of forethought (their surprise).

(*b*) Lack of clear ideas (about the Cross, even though so often told).

(*c*) Lack of knowledge of self (thought themselves strong).

(*d*) Lack of discipline (morally and spiritually raw).

2. **Its cure.** One thing needful—faith, *i.e.* trust in the Master.

(*a*) Faith gives forethought.

(*b*) Faith leads to clear insight.

(*c*) Faith brings knowledge of self.

(*d*) Faith develops experience.

15

THE DENIAL

PETER's denial of his Master was at once the climax of his sin and the occasion of a new start. It was therefore a pivot in his career, and demands very careful study, and, still more, very earnest meditation (see Matt. xxvi. 58, 69-75; Mark xiv. 54, 67-72; Luke xxii. 31f. and 54-63; John xviii, 15-18, 25-27).

A. THE PREDISPOSING CAUSES OF THE FALL

1. The sad facts

(*a*) Self-sufficiency. Due to: (1) Confidence and (2) Rashness (Prov. xxviii. 26).

(*b*) Partial knowledge. No Cross was contemplated by Peter. Christ's teaching had been entirely ignored.

(*c*) Spiritual negligence. Sleeping in Gethsemane. Then following "afar off" (cf. "also" in John xviii. 17, 25). John, bold and fearless, went in, and there was no need to ask the question of him. Peter remained behind and apart. He was "far off" from Christ and from his fellow-disciples, and among his Master's enemies. This is always dangerous.

2. The solemn lessons

(*a*) The fall is perfectly intelligible. It was no moral miracle or sudden and unexpected occurrence. It was due to predisposing conditions.

(*b*) "No one suddenly becomes base." The steps may be secret, but they exist. Every moment we are building up or weakening character.

B. THE ACTUAL CIRCUMSTANCES OF THE FALL

1. The full details

(*a*) Imagine an Oriental house with interior court like quadrangle. It had a passage from street to court by gateway. Inside the court was a fire.

(*b*) Three *periods* of denial rather than to three isolated and separate persons: (1) At the gate on entrance. (2) By the fire. (3) In the court by kinsman of Malchus.

(*c*) Three stages: (1) Evasion. (2) Oaths. (3) Passion.

2. The definite sins

(*a*) Falsehood.

(*b*) Ingratitude.

(*c*) Cowardice (dissimulation and simulation).

(*d*) Profanity.

(*e*) Persistence (three times).

3. The aggravating feature

(*a*) After great privileges.

(*b*) After strong protestations.

(*c*) After solemn warnings.

(*d*) In his Master's direst need.

Thus Peter sounded the depth of weakness and wickedness.

C. THE IMMEDIATE RESULTS OF
THE FALL

1. **The restoration.** Its course.

(*a*) An incident (cock-crowing). Slight and ordinary. God can use such.

(*b*) A look ("The Lord turned"). Consider what this conveyed: (1) Reminder. (2) Reproof. (3) Sorrow. (4) Entreaty.

(*c*) A memory. The past recalled.

(*d*) A thought. "I thought on my ways and turned" (Ps. cxix. 59; Luke xv. 17).

2. **The restoration.** Its reality.

(*a*) How proved? (1) Sorrow. (2) Deep sorrow ("bitterly"). (3) Immediate departure ("went out").

(*b*) Contrast with Judas. The same terms are used (in Greek). Yet what a difference! Judas lost his faith, then cast away his love, and went over to the enemy as a traitor. Peter thought to save himself without hurting Christ: selfish, weak, and wicked, but not apostate. Judas thought of the *consequence* of his sin, and so came remorse leading to despair. Peter thought of the sin itself, and so was led to repentance and hope. "Satan tripped Peter, but trapped Judas."

D. THE SIMPLE EXPLANATION OF
THE FALL

1. **The one great lack.** What he had lost— FAITH (cf. Luke xxii. 32). "That thy *faith* fail not," *i.e.* faith in his Master as Messiah and Son of

God (cf. Matt. xvi. 16). This was at the root of everything.

2. **The one great power**. What faith would have done. It would have
   (*a*) Enabled him to understand the Cross.
   (*b*) Given him strength of soul.
   (*c*) Developed his grateful love.
   (*d*) Inspired him with holy boldness.

3. **The one great secret**. How faith may be retained—"Abide in Me." Not "following afar off," but keeping close to our Lord.

THOUGHTS OF TEMPTATION

1. **The powers of prominence in the kingdom of God.**

2. **Satan's temptations are always directed towards God's children** (cf. Bible throughout). No need to tempt the worldling and unconverted. They go their own way without it.

3. **Our greatest danger is at our strongest (not our weakest) point** (cf. Abraham, faith, Gen. xii. 10-13; Moses, meekness, Num. xx. 10; Job, patience, Job iii. 1; Peter, self-confidence).

4. **God's provision is perfect, and "never need we yield."**

(*a*) "Armour of light" against the flesh (Rom. xii. 12).

(*b*) "Armour of righteousness" against the world (2 Cor. vi. 7).

(*c*) "Armour of God" against the devil (Eph. vi. 13).

16

STEPS UPWARD

PETER has sounded the lowest deeps. But he does
not remain there. After the fall he rises again, after
the wandering he returns, after the lapse comes a
fresh start. "Out of the depths" (Ps. cxxx. 1). Let
us now trace the steps upward.

A. REPENTANCE (Mark 14:72)

1. **Its unmistakable genuineness**
(*a*) Thought.
(*b*) Sorrow.
(*c*) Action.
Repentance includes all three elements, not merely the first two, which mean "penitence." Repentance
is "a change of mind which issues at once in a change
of life."

2. **Its apparent hopelessness.** Peter never expected the Resurrection and the sight of his
Master again—so that apparently the Denial was
his last act for his Lord! Thus he could not alter
matters, nor tell out his sorrow.

B. REMEMBERANCE (Mark 16:7)

1. **His Master's personal interest.** A special
message to him; "and Peter." An individual and
definite assurance.

2. **His Master's unchanging love.** The message reminded him that denial and death had made no difference in his Master's attitude.

C. RESTORATION
(Luke 24:34; 1 Cor. 15:5)

1. **The Master's tender consideration.** He saw his erring and sorrowing servant alone first, and so saved the embarrassment which would have otherwise arisen.

2. **The servant's deep contrition.** This can easily be imagined. We have no record of this, and rightly it is well hidden, for it was too sacred for words. "Something sealed the lips of that evangelist."

3. **The Saviour's healing love.** Imagine the word and touch of forgiveness and the healing balm of peace that followed.

D. REUNION (John 21:3,7)

1. **Waiting for the Master** (v. 3)

2. **Welcoming the Master** (v. 7)

How characteristic the action of Peter here! Going fishing while waiting. Plunging into the sea to reach the shore first and meet the Master.

E. REINSTATEMENT (John 21:15-19)

1. **The importance of the occasion**

(a) Its vivid reminders of the past. Contrast "after supper" John xiii. 2) and "when they had dined" (v. 15); "fire of coals" (John xviii. 18 and xxi. 9); threefold denial and threefold inquiry; references to sheep and shepherd (Matt. xxvi. and xxxi.).

(*b*) Its real necessity for the future. Public denial followed by public reinstatement. The *disciple* has been restored privately; the *apostle* must be restored publicly.

2. The first stage

(*a*) The question. (1) Its form. The old name (Simon). (2) Its meaning: "Lovest thou" [the real test] "Me" [personal devotion] "more than these?" *i.e.* than these disciples love Me (cf. the boast, Mark xiv. 29).

N.B.—The word for "love is *agapao,* an unselfish love, friendship-love.

(*b*) The answer. (1) Its form: Asseveration, "Yea"—"lovest." The word is *phileo,* a love which seeks return for affection. (2) Its meaning: Ernest, humble (he calls Christ to witness), and devoted.

(*c*) The commission. (1) Who? The "lambs" or young beginners. (2) What? "Feed," provide nourishment.

3. The second stage

(*a*) The question. (1) Its variation: The comparison with others is never omitted; yet the higher word for love is still used, *agapao.* (2) Its repetition, pressed as a test, "Do you love me?"

(*b*) The answer. (1) Its repetition. There is no change, for he has nothing else to say. (2) Its meaning: he is ready to meet the test.

(*c*) The commission. (1) Who? "Sheep," *i.e.* experienced believers. (2) What? Tend, *i.e.* do the work of a shepherd: guide, protect, provide.

4. The third stage

(*a*) The question. (1) Its significant change. Jesus now uses Peter's lower word for love, *phileo.*

(2) Its searching test: "Are you quite sure you have even this lower kind of love? Are you quite sure you are attached to Me? Quite sure you are a follower of Mine?" So our Lord sifts, not like Satan, to keep the chaff (Luke xxii. 31), but to preserve the wheat.

(*b*) The answer. (1) The feeling. "Grieved." Why? Because the third time Jesus used the lower word and questioned even *that*. (2) The response. Peter leaves it to Christ's perfect knowledge. How *can* He question it?

(*c*) The commission. (1) Who? "Sheeplings" (Greek, see R.V. and Westcott), *i.e.* between lambs and grown sheep. "Growing sheep." (2) What? "Feed." Need of growing Christians. We see here three stages of Christians, answering exactly to "children, fathers, and young men" (1 John ii. 12-14).

N.B.—Dwell on the words for "love" as here used, or the point will be lost: *agapao,* to love with a love which unselfishly expects nothing back; *phileo,* to love with a personal clinging affection which finds joy and satisfaction in returned love. The former is the higher, and hence the standard and test by our Lord. The latter is the lower, as Peter could not yet rise to the other. The grief (not the irritation) of Peter was that Jesus should doubt whether he possessed even the lower love.

SUGGESTIONS

1. Love is the supreme test of life.
2. Love to Christ is the essence of Christianity.
3. Love is only truly expressed in definite service.

17

LESSONS RESUMED

WE now gather up the concluding lessons of our Lord's earthly ministry with special reference to Simon Peter. They include teaching of the deepest importance in view of the future work of the now restored disciple and reinstated Apostle. Study John xxi., and see in it, especially in earliest verses, some of the great principles of all life and service.

A. LESSONS ON WORK (John 21:1-14)

This episode, as part of the appendix of the Gospel (xx. 30, 31), may be taken as a parable of what our Lord's attitude is now in relation to the whole Church and its work.

1. **The great pre-requisites of Christian work** (v. 2). Seven disciples are referred to; a microcosm of the whole Church, and suggesting—

(*a*) **Unity.** Some are named (prominent) some are unnamed (unknown); yet all are needed.

(*b*) **Variety.** Consider the temperaments as here represented. Impulse (Peter), doubt (Thomas), sincerity (Nathanael), sons of Zebedee (love). Work for God needs and can utilize all this unity and variety.

2. **The only call to work** (v. 3). Did Jesus order them to go fishing? Did He not tell them to wait? Was this the reason of their want of success? The call to work must come from Christ alone.

3. **The real encouragement in work** (vv. 4, 5). Jesus was on shore watching them in their toil. He inquired as to the results. His personal interest in what we do is the very best incentive to faithful service. "He saw them toiling in rowing" (Mark vi. 48).

4. **The true method of work** (v. 6). When and where He orders.

5. **The supreme secret of work** (v. 6). Prompt obedience.

6. **The varied characters in work** (vv. 7, 8). John is the first to recognize Christ (insight). Peter at once attempts to reach the shore (enthusiasm). The others bring the boats to land (ordinary work). Disciples of all sorts are needed and included in the Church.

1. **The blessed outcome of work** (vv. 9-14)

(*a*) The Master's preparation for them (v. 9).

(*b*) The Master's invitation (v. 10).

(*c*) The Master's welcome (v. 12).

(*d*) The Master's fellowship (v. 13).

So will it be hereafter (Matt. xxv. 34; Rev. xix. 9).

B. LESSONS ON CHARACTER (21:18-19)

In connection with the commission to Peter already considered (vv. 15-17) we find our Lord revealing to His servant some of the secrets of true service in the need of power and character and faithfulness. His whole life is laid open, and the true attitude of the disciple's future is contrasted with his past.

1. **Peter's past described** (v. 18)
(*a*) Impulse.
(*b*) Independence.

2. **Peter's future disclosed** (v. 18)
(*a*) Surrender.
(*b*) Suffering.
(*c*) Glory.

3. **Peter's present declared** (v. 19)
(*a*) Relationship.
(*b*) Loyalty.

N.B.—The importance of character in discipleship cannot be over-estimated. We "do" only in proportion to what we "are." "Thyself and doctrine" (1 Tim. iv. 16). "Good and faithful," *i.e.* good and therefore faithful (Matt. xxv. 21).

C. LESSONS ON DUTY (21:20-22)

Peter characteristically inquires about his friend John's future, and this becomes the occasion of further lessons for his life.

1. **Each servant of Christ has a supreme law:** "If I will."
(*a*) The Master's will always sovereign over all.
(*b*) The Master's will not always seen by all.

Peter was fond of meddling and even trying to "manage" his Master. But he learnt the lesson later (cf. 1 Pet. iv. 15, "busybody").

2. **Each servant of Christ has a special sphere**

(*a*) To one it is working (Peter).

(*b*) To another it is waiting (John).

Responsibilities, duties, etc., are *individual*. Separateness characterizes the Christian life in conversion, experience, growth, difficulties, sorrows, joys, blessings. "To every man *his* work" (Mark 13:34).

3. **Each servant of Christ has a simple duty**

(*a*) Absolute trust.

(*b*) Implicit obedience.

Active, energetic Christians are liable to exaggerate their own responsibilities. "They also serve who only stand and wait." To all comes the word, "Follow ME."

18

THE GREAT FORTY DAYS

THE time between the Resurrection and Ascension must have had a profound and important influence on Simon Peter's life. The appearances of our Lord and His instructions (Matt. xxviii. 19, 20; Mark xvi. 14, 15; Luke xxiv. 45-49; John xx. 19-23; Acts i. 3) enabled the Apostle to understand what before had been mysterious, and to enter more fully into His Master's purpose. Then came the ten days between Ascension and Pentecost. Study Acts i.

A. THE CLOSE OF THE MASTER'S EARTHLY MINISTRY (Acts 1:1-14)

1. **The Master's work** (vv. 2, 3)
(*a*) Commanding His Apostles.
(*b*) Confirming His resurrection.
2. **The Master's promise**
(*a*) The command to wait.
(*b*) The promise of power (cf. Acts ii. 33).
3. **The servant's ignorance** (v. 6)
(*a*) Old ideas persist long.
(*b*) Even after forty days' teaching.
4. **The Master's teaching** (vv.7, 8)

(*a*) Negative: Knowledge withheld.
(*b*) Positive: Power bestowed.
5. **The glorious Ascension** (vv. 9, 10)
(*a*) The departure of the Master.
(*b*) The interest of the disciples.
6. **The promised return** (vv. 10, 11)
(*a*) The angels' reproof.
(*b*) The angels' assurance.
7. **The disciples' attitude** (vv. 12-14)
(*a*) Joyful obedience (cf. Luke xxiv. 52 f.).
(*b*) Prayerful expectation.

B. THE COMMENCEMENT OF THE DISCIPLE'S MINISTRY (1:15-26)

1. **Peter's position** (v. 15)
(*a*) First on list of names—the leader—yet "in the midst." "Stood up." Was it quite wise? He had been told to wait!
(*b*) Note the consistency between the Peter of gospels and Acts. Prompt, energetic decision.
2. **His words about Judas.** Probably vv. 16 and 21 and 22 only are his, and vv. 18-20 the comment of Luke in explanation. Note the idea of "necessity" (vv. 16 and 22). Had Peter been instructed as to this?
3. **His counsel** (vv. 21, 22). Note the qualification of an apostle. Personal knowledge of Christ's earthly ministry and resurrection. These were unique and therefore impossible after that age.
4. **The action** (v. 23). Choice of two only. Why so limited? Were they the only two who fulfilled the qualifications?

5. **The prayer** (v. 24). They only prayed *after* they had chosen the two. Was this quite right? Why restrict God thus?

6. **The lot** (v. 26). It seems strange to read of companions of Jesus using this old-time method. It appears to show a lower plane of spiritual action than we might have expected. We never hear of it again. After this the Holy Spirit led them by spiritual perception and insight.

7. **The result:** "The lot fell." Note the vagueness of expression—no reference to God's action. Was Peter right? May not God have had His own way and time for filling up the gap by the choice of Paul? There are only "Twelve" foundations in the heavenly city (Rev. xxi.) It almost seems as if Peter had once again acted impulsively instead of simply "waiting," as his Master told him.

SUGGESTIONS

1. **Our great work.** Witnessing (v. 8). Distinguish between preaching and witnessing. The latter is marked by personal experience.

2. **Our great field.** The world (v. 8).

3. **Our great need.** Power (v. 8).

4. **Our great provision.** The Holy Spirit (v. 8).

5. **Our great secret.** Waiting on God; receiving from God. "Stand still." We have need of quiet and repose of soul. Then will come simple faith and loving obedience.

19

PENTECOSTAL POWER

The Day of Pentecost was a pivot in Peter's life. It is important to mark the great and even astonishing contrasts. Previously he had been unbalanced, blundering, a mixture of cowardice and confidence, of good impulses and great mistakes. Now he is strong, sober-minded, courageous. How is the difference accounted for? We may find it in the days of preparation after the Resurrection, crowned by the Day of Pentecost.

We now study Acts ii. so far as it concerns Peter.

A. THE MAN (Acts 2:14)

1. Note his promptitude.
2. Mark his boldness.
3. Consider his clearness. R.V., "spake forth."

B. THE MESSAGE (2:14-40)

Study this carefully as the *first* Christian sermon. It is also valuable as an instance of a Jewish Christian addressing non-Christian Jews with a view to conviction.

1. **Its assertions.** To refute (vv. 14-21).

(*a*) Negatively (vv. 14, 15). Accusation repelled.

(*b*) Positively (vv. 16-21). Acquaintance with Scripture.

2. Its arguments. To convince (vv. 22-36).

(*a*) The work of Jesus (vv. 22-32). (1) His life (v. 22). (2) His death (v. 23). (3) His resurrection (v. 24-32).

(*b*) The glory of Jesus (vv. 33-36). (1) Exalted by God (v. 33). (2) Acknowledged by God (v. 33). (3) Honored by God (vv. 34-36). (4) Rejected by man (v. 36).

3. Its appeal. To lead (v. 37-40).

(*a*) Conviction.

(*b*) Direction.

(*c*) Exhortation.

N.B.—This sermon is deserving of the closest attention by all Christian preachers,[1] and hence we proceed to consider—

C. THE MEANING

1. The substance of true preaching

(*a*) What it is. The Lord Jesus Christ in His— (1) Person. (2) Work. (3) Claim on man.

(*b*) How it should be stated. (1) Clearly—in its simplicity and definiteness. (2) Completely—in its facts, commands, and promises.

2. The wisdom of true preaching

(*a*) In presenting the message. Note Jesus as "man" first (v. 22), with the facts known to and acknowledged by all. Then only gradually led up to Jesus as "Messiah" at the close (v. 36). The *way* we present the message counts for much.

---

[1] See, further, Stifler's *Introduction to the Book of Acts* and *Commentary on Acts,* by David Thomas, D.D. Published by Kregel Publications.

(*b*) In winning the attention. He appealed to their own Scriptures and gave proofs. This would impress them. Note this careful arrangement of his matter:

First, the acknowledged fact of Christ's life: "Ye know" (v. 22).

Second, the argument from Scripture.

Third, the events of that day, Pentecost.

Thus the *strongest* argument comes first, the *most difficult* second, and the *most impressive* last.[1] Whence this remarkable power in Peter?

3. **The elements of true preaching**

(*a*) In the man. (1) Confidence in the truth. (2) Authoritativeness. (3) Sympathy. (4) Tact (5) Faithfulness. (6) Earnestness. (7) Spirituality.

N.B.—Draw out all these from the record of Peter's address.

(*b*) In the message. (1) Based on Scripture. (2) Supported by sound arguments. (3) Witnessed to by simple facts. (4) Characterized by clear doctrine. (5) Suffused by personal experience. (6) Marked by practical definiteness, leading to immediate decision.

CONCLUSION

In all preaching the Son of God is the substance, the Word of God is the instrument, the Spirit of God is the power, the Man of God is the channel, the salvation of God is the result, and the glory of God is the end.

[1] See Stifler *in loco*.

20

ORDINARY LIFE

AFTER the great event of Pentecost comes the quiet routine of daily life followed by manifestation of miraculous power. Study Acts iii. for its notable additional revelations of Peter's character.

A. THE APOSTLE'S DAILY LIFE (Acts 3:1-5)

1. **Fellowship realized** (v. 1). "Peter and John." Christianity is not a solitary and purely individualistic religion.

2. **Worship required** (v. 1). "To pray." Worship is a necessary expression of true life.

3. **Need revealed** (vv. 2-5). It was impossible for them to be indifferent to the needs of those around.

B. THE APOSTLE'S SPECIAL POWER
(3:6-11)

1. **Claimed** (v. 6). Notice the reference to Jesus as "of Nazareth."

2. **Shared** (v. 7)

(*a*) By sympathy, "took him by the right hand."

(*b*) By help, "lifted him up."

3. **Proved** (vv. 8-11)

(*a*) By the man.
(*b*) To the people.

C. THE APOSTLE'S FAITHFUL PREACHING (3:12-16)

The astonishment of the multitude gave Peter his opportunity, and right well he used it. Note the element of his testimony.

1. **Man was disclaimed** (v. 12). "Why attend to us? Ours is not the power."

2. **God was honored** (vv. 13-15). Note carefully the fourfold statement of their sin and its climax: (1) "Ye delivered up." (2) "Ye denied." (3) Ye desired a murderer." (4) "Ye killed the Prince of Life." But God glorified Him by raising Him up.

3. **Explanation was afforded** (v. 16).

(*a*) The name of Jesus (*i.e.* His character and power) as the source of blessing.

(*b*) Faith in Him as the channel of blessing.

Then Peter is led on further, and we notice—

D. THE APOSTLE'S WISE ATTITUDE (3:17-26)

He longs to win them to his Master. This introduces us to a spiritual miracle as great as the other. Note the masterliness of the now transformed man.

1. **Loving extenuation** (vv. 17, 18). Human ignorance does not mean human innocence. The Divine overruling was the door of hope to them.

2. **Earnest exhortation** (v. 19) (see R.V., "Repent and turn"). The phrase "be converted" of

the A.V. is liable to misconception. Repentance is a change of mind which leads the soul to "turn." It means a change of thought or mind which leads at once to change of will and conduct.

3. **Gracious promises** (vv. 19, 20) (see R.V., not A.V., here) (1) Sins blotted out. (2) Seasons of refreshing. (3) Sending the Messiah.

4. **Clear prophecies** (vv. 21-24). Their Scriptures are again used. Note the meaning of "restitution of all things." It is limited and explained by "whereof God hath spoken by the mouth of His holy prophets."

5. **Personal application** (v. 25). "Yet."

6. **Divine assurance** (v. 26). God's love is declared.

N.B.—Study this able and powerful address in fullest detail. A remarkable combination of intellectual force and spiritual power.

SUGGESTIONS

Some personal characteristics of a Spirit-filled man.

1. **Sympathy** (v. 4). "Fastening his eyes." Thus the lame man was led to expectation. So sympathy always will show itself, and influence others.

2. **Frankness** (v. 6). No money. Imagine the disappointment of the mendicant!

3. **Boldness** (v. 9). His great claim for Jesus of Nazareth. Suppose the possibility of failure! What ignominy would have resulted!

4. Humility (v. 12). "Yet not I" (cf. 1 Cor. xv. 10).

5. Faithfulness (vv. 13-16). Their sin is plainly declared. Fidelity is always truest kindness.

6. Generosity (v. 17). He made the best of their position.

7. Tactfulness (vv. 22-26). He tries to win support by using their Scriptures. And the tone and substance of his address is loving and attractive. Manner counts for much in work. Tone and spirit mean very much. "Impertinence is not faithfulness," neither is hardness of attitude.

CONCLUSIONS

How came these new and strange elements in Peter?

1. **The Spirit was guiding into all truth** (John xvi. 13); hence the clearness of teaching. The Master, the Word, the Spirit, thus filled the disciple and used him to the glory of God.

2. **The Spirit was glorifying Jesus to him** (John xvi. 14); hence the mellowness of soul.

21

OPPOSITION

BLESSING is always followed closely by testing, and soon after Peter's address (Acts iii.), following the miracle, the first opposition to the Gospel was experienced, and the first conflict with outside foes. Study Acts iv., and note Peter's attitude and spirit throughout the trying experiences.

A. SUFFERING FOR THE TRUTH (Acts 4:1-7)

1. **Opposition** (vv. 1, 2). Two grounds.

(*a*) Teaching the people (the Apostles being unauthorized and unofficial).

(*b*) Proclaiming the Resurrection, and associating it with Jesus (Sadducees did not accept Resurrection at all).

2. **Imprisonment** (v. 3). Yet even at that time blessing was vouchsafed (v. 4).

3. **Trial** (vv. 5-7). Note the inquiry. They asked the power and authority of the Apostles.

B. TESTIMONY TO THE TRUTH (4:8-12)

1. **Its one secret** (v. 8): "Filled with the Holy Ghost." This is the secret of the only effective witness.

2. **Its glorious message** (vv. 9-12); Christ.
(*a*) The power of Christ (vv. 9, 10).
(*b*) The glory of Christ (v. 11).
(*c*) The salvation of Christ (v. 12).

3. **Its true spirit** (v. 10). Courage. See the boldness in every line: "Be it known"; "Ye crucified"; "Set at nought of you builders"; "None other name."

C. IMPRESSION OF THE TRUTH
(4:13-18)

1. **Astonishment** (v. 13)
(*a*) Because of their boldness, though ignorant men.
(*b*) Because of their association with Jesus.
This combination of boldness with Jesus.
was also seen in Jesus, and probably was remembered by the rulers (Mark vi. 2; Matt. vii. 28-29; John vii. 15).

2. **Perplexity** (v. 14). "Facts are stubborn things' (cf. John xi. 47).

3. **Proposal** (vv. 16-18). They decided to silence the Apostles. A strangely inept and ineffectual policy.

D. CONTENTION FOR THE TRUTH
(4:19-22)

Peter's tone increases in boldness.

1. **The supreme claim** (v. 19). God must be put and kept first.

2. **The strong constraint** (v. 20). "We cannot but speak."

3. **The striking confession** (vv. 21, 22)

(*a*) Inability to punish.

(*b*) Ineffectual threats.

E. FELLOWSHIP IN THE TRUTH
(4:23-32)

On their release their action is noteworthy.

1. **Spiritual affinity** (v. 23). "To their own company." How natural, inevitable, beautiful! They followed the law of spiritual crystallization. Contrast the darker side, "his own place" (Acts i. 25).

2. **United prayer** (vv. 24-30). Mark the unselfish character of the petitions. They asked not for protection or preservation, but for more power to witness.

3. **Divine blessing** (vv. 31-33). The answer came in increased power, further testimony, and deeper blessing.

SUGGESTIONS

1. **Peter's attitude.** The exhibition.

(*a*) Clear testimony: (1) To Jesus, by word. (2) To Jesus, by life.

N.B.—Something in Peter clearly reminded them of Jesus. Do we remind people of Him?

(*b*) Unflinching courage.

(*c*) Strong character.

2. **Peter's ability.** The explanation.

(*a*) God was real (v. 19).

(*b*) Christ was precious (vv. 10-12).

(*c*) The Spirit was powerful (v. 8).

22

APOSTOLIC DISCIPLINE

In Acts iv. 31-33 we see a beautiful picture of the Church as a whole indwelt by the Holy Spirit. We now proceed to the study of the first instances and illustrations of *individual* Christian life in relation to the presence of the Spirit of God. The study must of necessity be mainly in connection with the Apostle Peter and his position and action. Study Acts iv. 34 to v. 16.

A. THE APOSTLE'S SPECIAL POSITION
(Acts 4:35-37)

1. **Consider the unique authority of the Apostles** (cf. vv. 35, 37: "laid it at the Apostles' feet"; v. 26, "surnamed by the Apostles"). They were at this time evidently the spiritual and temporal guides of the infant Church. This unique position was thus clearly acknowledged by the Church and accepted by it, and as clearly authority was exercised by the Apostles. Collect the references to "the Apostles" and "the Twelve" first in the Gospels, then in the Acts, and then in the Epistles, to see this authority very definitely. Yet it was manifestly exceptional, and intended only for the foundation of the

Church (Eph. ii. 20). As Apostles they had, and
could have, no successors. The qualification for
Apostleship was unique and necessarily limited
(Acts i. 21, 22).

2. **Dwell on the action of Barnabas.** His discipleship had developed along the line of the gift
of teaching, and was designated for this work by
the Apostles (Eph. iv. 11, "some pastors and
teachers"). (Bar-nabas, Son of Encouragement,
Consolation.) A man of substance, he spontane-
ously sold his property and gave the money for
the good of the Church. His action is thus in
marked contrast to what follows (cf. "But," ch.
v. 1).

B. THE APOSTLE'S SPIRITUAL PERCEPTION
(5:1-4)

1. **The sin.** Ananias in appearance did the same
as Barnabas, *but* in reality what a difference! Sin
of avarice on the surface; deep still, hypocrisy—
the appearance of consecration without the genuine
experience.

2. **The detection** (v. 3). Note Peter's supernatural knowledge, taught by the Spirit. The sin
is traced to its sources (Satan, v. 3; self, v. 4).
The will always yields, and is never overcome.
If Satan is resisted he always flees (1 Pet. v. 9).
Note the awfulness of the sin in the way it is
characterized. In *purpose* it was to "lie to the Holy
Ghost" (v. 3), or to "cheat the Holy Ghost." In *act*
it was "lying not to men, but to God." The person-
ality and Godhead of the Holy Spirit are clearly

taught by Peter's words, and also his immediate superintendence of the Church as "the executive of the Godhead." Without another moment Ananias fell down dead; there was no opportunity for exhortation or repentance. The judgment of God descended swiftly, and visited his sin on him. No word or act of Peter caused this, but "an act of God."

C. THE APOSTLE'S SEARCHING PROOF
(5:8)

Again the authority of Peter's apostleship was exercised.

1. **Note his significant question:** "Did ye sell the land for so much?" What is meant by "so much"?

(1) He may have heard of the actual and full price received, and by confronting her with this information intended to probe her conscience and remind her that all was known; (2) or the money actually laid at the Apostle's feet may have still been there, and "so much" referred to that. In either case it would have been a question to search and try.

2. **Consider the shameless answer.** She answers simply, "Yea, for so much," and in either meaning of the phrase her guilt is the same. Her lying is deliberate and even defiant. *Suppressio veri suggestio falsi.*

D. THE APOSTLE'S SOLEMN
PREROGATIVE (5:9-10)

1. **He administered a rebuke.** "Why have ye agreed together to tempt the Spirit of God?"

Here and in v. 2 we see clearly the wife's conni-
vance and co-operation. When a wife thus
furthers her husband's sinful projects he is much
more likely to descend to evil, just as a man
helped towards good by his wife is at a great advantage. God has placed wonderful power in
woman's hands.

2. **He declared God's judgment.** In this case
Peter *declares* what was to take place, and at once
the judgment takes effect. It is immediately exe-
cuted by the Divine Hand, and soon the wife is
lying in the grave side by side with her husband and
partner in sin. Why was this terrible severity? It
was demanded by the circumstances. The Church
was in its infancy, and everything depended on its
life. Hence the need of a deep impression as to what
sin meant, what the holiness of God meant, and what
the immediate rulership of the Holy Ghost meant.
Israel was taught similar lessons in its early days in
the sin of the Golden Calf (Exod. xxxii. 27, 28) and
in the sin of Nadab and Abihu (Num. iii. 4). God
will be sanctified in those who come near Him (Lev.
x. 3).

E. THE APOSTLE'S SUPERNATURAL
POWER (5:11-16)

The result of this striking experience was very
remarkable. Through the terrible purging came
increased power.

1. **Note the godly fear** (vv. 5, 11, 13). Awe
fell on the Church and on all around. They real-

ized what God was. "Holy and reverend is His name" (Ps. cxi. 9).

2. **Mark the spiritual influence:** (v. 12), many miracles by the Apostles; (v. 13), testimony by the populace; (v. 14), great additions to the Church; (v. 15), remarkable influence of Peter; (v. 16), blessing spreading to the country districts. Thus did God overrule sin to His own glory.

SUGGESTIONS

1. **An awful danger: spiritual pretence in the Church.** Avarice was not the only or deepest sin in this instance. The real sin was a *desire to be thought a saint,* to be regarded as wholly consecrated when they were not. This sin of pretended sanctity takes various forms, and is possible quite apart from money. Exaggeration of our gifts or, the contrary, minimizing our means of giving is in principle the sin of Ananias. Giving the impression of doing our utmost when we know we have not is the same root evil. So with our worship, our time, and in other ways. There is special danger of this in times of revival—of being in the midst of spiritual blessing without being partakers of it, and yet speaking and acting *as though we were.* Temptation to galvanize our life into spiritual force. The danger of pretended holiness is most perilous.

2. **A wonderful provision: spiritual perception in the Church.** Note Peter's detection of the sin. Even apart from miraculous gifts, a great deal of spiritual perception is possible. It is the result

of fellowship with God, and is the mark of a growing experience. Note Phil. i. 10: Greek, "discern things that differ" (see Heb. v. 14, "senses exercised by reason of use to discern"). Study carefully the later Epistles of Paul, Peter, and John, and see the emphasis on "knowledge" and "know and note especially the characteristic of the mature Christians (the "fathers" in 1 John ii. 14) is that they *"know"* (cf. Phil. i. 9, Greek, and Col. i. 9). Such "perception" saves from error, and enables us to "try the spirits" (1 John iv. 1, 2 and ii. 20).

3. **An absolute necessity: spiritual purity in the Church.** God is holy, therefore must His people be holy. A Church can be spoilt by one or two members, and blessing withheld (cf. Achan, Joshua vii).

4. **A blessed experience: spiritual power in the Church.** After purity came power. The power of Satan and self (vv. 3, 4) gave place to the power of the Spirit. The spirit of love triumphed over avarice, the spirit of truth over hypocrisy, the spirit of holiness over sin, and the Church went forward blessed and made a blessing.

23

BEFORE THE COUNCIL AGAIN

THE great influence and blessing following the trouble about Ananias and Sapphira could not but attract attention of the Jewish authorities, and compel them to move. Study carefully Acts v. 17-42; note the details, especially as they bear on Peter's attitude and character. Three forces were represented in the persons of the High Priest, Gamaliel, and Peter.

A. THE SPIRIT OF ERROR
(The High Priest)

1. **Note the malignant hostility:** v. 17, indignation (R.V., jealousy); v. 33, "minded to slay them."

2. **See the appeal to force:** v. 18, "prison." Why not argue the matter first? Their only argument was "might is right."

3. **Mark the manifest fear:** v. 24, R.V., "perplexed." Evidently they were impressed by the miraculous deliverance from prison.

4. **Consider the cowardly insincerity** (v. 28). Note the absence of all reference whatever to the event recorded in v. 19. It was convenient to ignore that. "This Man's blood": they will not refer by name to Jesus.

N.B.—How far the enmity of the human heart to God will go! Such passages as Rom. viii. 7, Eph. ii. 1-3, are not for the past only, but for all time.

B. THE SPIRIT OF COMPROMISE
(Gamaliel)

1. **The counsel was marked by great plausibility.** Time *does* test things. So far Gamaliel was true, but it was not the whole truth. Many erroneous systems have lasted for centuries, but are not thereby proved to be "of God."

2. **It was characterized by utter falsity.** Time is not the only test. How can we wait until the end before testing reality? In the course of the history we *must* put things to the proof.

3. **It was stamped with manifest indifference.** Gamaliel had a moral obligation to test the evidence for Christianity; so have all earnest men. It is impossible to be neutral if we are in earnest; we must be for or against.

4. **It really revealed essential moral cowardice.** If Gamaliel had proved Christianity to be of God, it would have involved taking sides and accepting Christ, or deliberately rejecting Him. He never seems to have had any intention of doing this.

N.B.—Compromise may sometimes be necessary and wise for sake of peace, providing it is never at the expense of truth (cf. Acts xvi. 3 with Gal. ii. 3-5). Now turn to a very different attitude.

C. THE SPIRIT OF TRUTH (Peter)

He is the spokesman for the rest (see Greek of "answered and, said," v. 29).

1. Fearlessness

(*a*) Commanded by God (v. 20).

(*b*) Manifested by Apostles: v. 21, they went into the Temple; v. 29, R.V., "we must." Cf. the answer in iv. 20, "we cannot but speak"—the human side, love; here "we must"—the Divine side, loyalty. Duties never conflict.

2. Faithfulness

(*a*) In proclaiming God's work: vv. 30-32, "*God* raised," "*God* exalted," "*God* gave."

(*b*) In declaring human sin: v. 30, "Ye slew and hanged . . ." Though a prisoner, he tells the authorities their sin.

N.B.—They had charged the Apostles with (1) disobedience and (2) bringing the death of Jesus on them. Peter thus meets these by (1) claiming to obey God rather than them, (2) charging the guilt of Jesus' death on them.

N.B.—Consider this splendid c o u r a g e and strength in the light of the denial. What a transformation of Divine grace! Yet side by side notice another quality—

3. Tactfulness

(*a*) He shows true conciliation even as he stands firm: v. 30, "The God of *our fathers*." He associates himself with them; he is no enemy of his nation. What had been done had been done by the God Whom he and they worshipped and honored.

(*b*) He affords them opportunity of salvation even as he denounces their sin: v. 31, "Exalted to give repentance to *Israel* and remission of sins." Even they might be saved.

N.B.—Mark this tenderness even in faithfulness, and dwell on this remarkable balance and combination of qualities in the formerly unbalanced and erratic Peter. Christian workers need both elements. Faithfulness alone might lead to severity and repulsion. Tactfulness alone might degenerate into weakness or craftiness; but together they do God's work effectively.

Once again the speech of Peter returns to the stronger side, and we notice—

4. Resoluteness

(*a*) He stands as a "witness of these things" (v. 32; cf. Acts i. 8).

(*b*) He actually associates himself and the others with the Holy Ghost (v. 32). What spiritual dignity is here! Was he justified in this bold collocation of "we" and the "Holy Ghost"? His Master's words are the justification (John xv. 26 f., R.V.): "The Spirit of truth . . . shall bear witness, and ye also shall bear witness" (cf. Acts. xv. 28, "It seemed good to us and to the Holy Ghost").

N.B.—Study well this answer of Peter. How concise, clear, definite, loving, faithful, and manly! See in it a fulfilment of Matt. x. 18-20.

5. Steadfastness

Although beaten by the authorities and ordered not to preach again, see the real spirit of the men.

(*a*) Their feeling and its cause: v. 41, "Exulting because counted worthy to suffer dishonor for the Name" (R.V.).

(*b*) Their action and its nature: v. 42, "Ceased not to teach . . . Jesus as the Christ" (R.V.).

SUGGESTIONS

Review Peter's action and note his condition. He was in an attitude of spiritual readiness for this emergency (see 1 Pet. iii. 15). He manifested this remarkable preparedness of speech and action because of the preparation of heart by the Spirit (Prov. xvi. 1).

1. The believer's only safety

(*a*) In speech bold: no uncertain sound.

(*b*) In heart courageous: no uncertain conviction.

(*c*) In will determined: no uncertain strength.

(*d*) In soul trustful: no uncertain confidence.

2. The believer's only secret

(*a*) God powerful (vv. 29-31).

(*b*) Christ precious (vv. 31, 42): "Prince," "Saviour," "the Messiah," "the Name."

(*c*) The Holy Spirit possessed (v. 32).

24

SIMON PETER AND SIMON MAGNUS

AFTER the return from the Council (Acts v. 41f.) Peter was occupied with the first internal problem of the infant Church (Acts vi. 1-4). The solution of this led to another persecution, culminating in the death of Stephen and dispersion of the Church of Jerusalem, with the exception of the Apostles (vi. 5 and viii. 4). Now we are concerned with the beginning of the Church in Samaria and of Peter's position in relation thereto, and especially to Simon Magus. Study Acts viii. 9-25, and note each stage very carefully.

A. SIMON MAGUS AND THE EVANGELIST
(Acts 8:9-13)

1. **Simon Magus' influence was great** (vv. 9, 10). Evidently he was more than a mere trickster. Some satanic arts seem to account for his power.

2. **Simon's influence weakened and neutralized by the Gospel** (v. 11). A "great power" met by a greater (Luke xi. 21f.).

3. **Simon's influence transformed** (v. 13). "Simon also himself believed." The most signal triumph of all. Notice three things said of him: (*a*) He accepted Christ—"believed" and "was

baptized." (*b*) He continued with Philip. (*c*) He was amazed at Philip's power. There is nothing to object to in anything here.

N.B.—This verse should be read from the standpoint of Luke writing of the event years after, and stating definitely, "Simon also believed." Why must we differentiate between vv. 12 and 13 as to belief? Why not take it as it stands, and read the rest of the story in the light of it? It is plainly stated that Simon fulfilled the conditions of Mark xvi. 16 (first clause). Why then doubt the results?

B. SIMON MAGUS AND THE APOSTLES
(8:14-17)

1. **The tidings of blessing came to Jerusalem** "Samaria had received the Word of God." This was a significant extension of Christianity beyond Judaism. A reminder of Acts i. 8.

2. **The action taken** shows the importance with which the event was regarded. Sent their leading Apostles. Note "they sent," *i.e.* Peter and John as deputation. There is no supremacy of Peter here. It sheds a clear light on his relation to other Apostles. They acted together as a body.

3. **The blessing bestowed** on the Samaritan Christians is very noteworthy.

(*a*) Clearly it was separate from the normal Christian experience of the reception of the Spirit at conversion according to ii. 38. An instance of miraculous gifts not ordinary grace.

(*b*) Manifestly it was an unique gift through the Apostles which Philip could not bestow. It testifies to the uniqueness of the Apostles herein. No others could do this. See Paul's power in xix. 6. Ananias in ix. 17 is no real exception.

(c) Evidently it was a miraculous and special attestation of work in Samaria, recognizing them as part of the Christian Church.

N.B.—This limitation of unique power to Apostles shows the impossibility of any "Apostolic succession." Such claims could only be proved today by similar "apostolic success."

C. SIMON MAGUS AND SIMON PETER
(8:18-24)

1. **The request** (vv. 18, 19). Simon Magus was deeply impressed. His antecedents fostered the feeling. It is easy to blame him, but it was very natural considering his past. It was a sudden temptation along old lines.

N.B. — This gift clearly came *through* the Apostles, and not direct from heaven, as at Pentecost (ii. 2, 33) and at Caesarea (x. 44). Here it was mediated through them.

2. **The rebuke** (vv. 20-23)

(a) Peter's characteristic vehemence (v. 20). He was horrified.

(b) "This matter," *i.e.* of the supernatural gifts of the Spirit. There is no necessary reference to Simon's own salvation (v. 21).

(c) Peter counsels him to "Repent" and "Pray" (v. 22), and suggests only the possibility of forgiveness ("if"), in case his repentance and prayer are not genuine and deep. Note "thought" in singular, *i.e.* the *one sin* of which he had just been guilty.

(*d*) Peter warns him of his danger (v. 23). See R.V. margin and Greek. Not *"in* the gall," but *"towards,"* "in the direction of" (Greek *into,* not *in*). "Gall of bitterness" is the wretchedness caused by sin; "bond of iniquity" the dominion leading to wretchedness.

N.B.—Ponder carefully the above, and consider Simon Magus's spiritual condition. *Was it hypocrisy or backsliding?* We think the latter is more agreeable to the story here given. For consider the following: (1) Verse, 13 clearly states he "believed," "was baptized," and "continued."

(2) Is Peter's counsel really appropriate to an unconverted man and a hypocrite? Would any worker today tell such an one to "repent" and "pray"? Yet Peter's words are exactly suited to a backslider.

(3) Note Peter's warning of his danger *"towards* the gall," etc., which shows he had not yet reached it.

(4) Consider Simon Magus's reply in v. 24.

3. **The result** (v. 24). Simon Magus fears the results, evidently believing them possible. He acknowledges "the Lord," and asks for prayer. Is this the language and attitude of an utterly base man? Surely it indicates an impression and a fear, with a desire for preservation from results of sin! Motives may not always be high, but God saves on any real motive. The story closes hopefully, and we may safely keep strictly and solely to Scripture, and leave later tradition alone.

N.B.—Contrast Paul's stern and unmistakable language to a sorcerer who *was* a scoundrel in xiii. 6-12. Peter would scarcely have dealt very differently with Simon Magus if he had been other than a backslider.

SUGGESTIONS

1. The possibility of backsliding

(*a*) Old temptation transformed. Simon inevitably thought of the former "wonders," and so was led astray.

(*b*) Old habits powerful. Instances are not rare of converted drunkards falling, temporarily into the old sin, though their true conversion had not been doubted. Regeneration is not renovation. Habits are still there. The young Christian is only a babe.

(*c*) Old desires active. Avarice, popularity, power.

2. The treatment of backsliding

(*a*) Strong emphasis on God's holiness (v. 20).

(*b*) Thorough faithfulness in personal dealing (v. 21).

(*c*) Earnest encouragement to repentance (vv. 22, 23).

3. The protection against backsliding

(*a*) The Spirit of truth. Teaching young converts.

(*b*) The Spirit of holiness. Creating sensitiveness against sin.

(*c*) The Spirit of power. Triumphing over the old nature.

25

PERSONAL MINISTRY

OUR studies of Simon Peter in the Acts have hitherto dealt with him in his public capacity as an Apostle
guiding and influencing the Church. But in Acts ix.
32-43 we see the more personal and individual side
of his ministry, and again thereby still more insight
into his character. Here he exercises personal ministry to individuals.

A. APOSTOLIC DUTY (Acts 9:32)

1. **What he did.** He visited from place to place
superintending the Churches. This was possible
through the political and social quiet then reign-
ing (v. 31). How came the Gospel in these parts?
Doubtless through Philip. See viii. 40, and note
map for route and places. Now came Apostolic
supervision by Peter as at Samaria (viii.).

2. **Why he came.** Lydda was (and still is) a
village nine miles east of Joppa on the way to
Jerusalem (Lod, 1 Chron. viii. 12). Religion is
thus found in an unexpected place. Note the term
"saints." Its first occurrence in this chapter as a
designation of Christians (vv. 13, 32, 41). It
means "consecrated" (cf. Rom. i. 7) or belonging
to God. Peter's spiritual affinity naturally led

him to the "saints" (cf. iv. 23); "their own company." He would not only give, but get, refreshment thereby.

B. PERSONAL WORK (9:33-35)

1. **A case of need** (v. 33). Great and prolonged sickness and disease (cf. Mark ii. 1 f.) Was Æneas a Christian? Most probably, for: (1) He seems to be among the saints. (2) No questions or conditions of healing are put. (3) The name of Jesus is apparently quite familiar.

2. **A bestowal of blessing** (v. 34). From Christ direct, immediate, and complete. Then comes the call to prove it by arising and making the bed, which was responded to immediately.

3. **A means of influence** (v. 35). Conviction ("saw") and then conversion ("turned") followed this miracle. "Sharon" (R.V.) is the maritime plain from Carmel to Joppa.

C. SPIRITUAL POWER (9:36-43)

1. **The great sorrow** (vv. 36-38)

(*a*) The fact of discipleship (v. 36). Christianity is found here also.

(*b*) The proof of discipleship (v. 36). Good works.

(*c*) The influence of discipleship (v. 37 f.) Loss and sorrow realized.

2. **The earnest call** (vv. 38, 39)

(*a*) They felt the need of Peter.

(*b*) They sent an urgent message.

(*c*) They received a prompt response.

3. **The suggestive revelation** (v. 40). Note a striking similarity to the circumstances of raising of Jairus' daughter (Mark v. 40-43). Peter closely follows his Master.

(*a*) The solitude: "Put them all forth."

(*b*) The prayer: "Kneeled . . . prayed."

(*c*) The expectation: "Turned . . . arise."

The prayer marks difference between Master and disciple (cf. Elisha in 2 Kings iv. 33, and Elijah in 1 Kings xvii. 20, 21). Note the similarity in "Tabitha, arise," and "Talitha,. arise" (Aramaic, *Kumi*). Peter would be clearly reminded of the earlier incident.

4. **The significant action** (v. 41)

(*a*) Sympathy: "Gave her his hand."

(*b*) Strength: "Raised her up."

(*c*) Satisfaction: "Presented her alive."

5. **The blessed results** (v. 42f.)

(*a*) Knowledge: "Became known."

(*b*) Faith: "Believed."

(*c*) Fellowship: "He abode."

SUGGESTIONS

1. Some characteristics of personal ministry

(*a*) Genuine and devoted activity. Peter was never idle or "unemployed."

(*b*) Blessed opportunities along life's daily path faithfully utilized.

(*c*) Specially interested in fellow Christians (v. 32). Look out for solitary Christians or small bodies, and show all possible fellowship.

(*d*) Touched by human need (v. 33). An eye to see and a heart to feel.

(*e*) Prompt response to call of sorrow and loss (v. 39). "Comfort" is specially needed in the work of the ministry (2 Cor. i. 4).

(*f*) Everything done in entire dependence on Divine power (v. 40; John xv. 5; Phil. iv. 13).

(*g*) Showing the most beautiful and tender thoughtfulness (v. 41). Not only doing great things but *little* things well. Mark this transformation of grace in one so different before Pentecost.

2. **Some secrets of personal ministry**

(*a*) The reality of the Master (v. 34). Christ realized as living, present, and mighty. So in all work the living Lord is the secret (cf. Mark xvi. 20, "The Lord working with them").

(*b*) The reality of prayer (v. 40). Prayer is power. "To pray is to labor (*Orare est laborare*) is much truer than "to labor is to pray" (Mark ix. 29; Matt. ix. 38).

26

SURPRISING LESSONS

ANOTHER Church problem soon arose, one of great magnitude and difficulty. It concerned the relation of Gentiles to Christianity. Were they to be included? And on what terms? All this involved new lessons for Peter; and in Acts x. 1—xi. 18 we have the record. The great detail given shows the importance with which the event was regarded. Consider it now mainly from Peter's standpoint, and watch for every indication of his character and spirit. The subject, moreover, needs full consideration as a whole.

A. THE APOSTLE'S PREPARATION
(Acts 10:9-16)

1. **The occasion** (vv. 9, 10). Note the conditions of soul (prayer), of body (hunger), of mind (trance).

2. **The vision** (vv. 11, 12). The vessel (*a*) was from God; (*b*) contained all sorts. A reminder of the Divine source and uniform value of all things therein. The old distinction of clean and unclean no longer held good.

3. **The command** (vv. 13, 14). Peter's hunger is used as a medium of the teaching. But he declines. "Not so, Lord." How like the natural

temperament of the Peter of the Gospels! (cf. Matt. xvi. 22; John xiii. 8).

4. **The lesson** (v. 15). See R.V. "Make," not "call." *When* did God "cleanse"? Then, or some time before? See R.V. of Mark viii. 19 (cf. Mark vii. 2, ff. May not God have referred back to our Lord's abolition of the distinction between clean and unclean? Note the threefold repetition of the vision to impress and confirm Peter.

B. THE APOSTLE'S ACTION (10:17-24)

1. **The perplexity** (v. 17). Peter gave the vision very careful thought.

2. **The summons** (vv. 17, 18). Note the exact coincidence of time.

3. **The assurance** (vv. 19, 20). Another coincidence in God's interposition. "The Spirit said" (cf. viii. 29). God's command and encouragement blend to confirm His servant.

4. **The response** (vv. 21-24). Hospitality offered and journey next day. Note the wisdom in taking others with him for confirmation. Whole-hearted and prompt obedience is so characteristic of Peter!

C. THE APOSTLE'S ATTITUDE (10:25-33)

Mark carefully the revelations of character here. How wonderfully God's grace was at work!

1. **Genuineness** (v. 26). True humility. Probably the "worship" only meant profound respect and homage (cf. our use of "Your Worship"). Yet it was felt by Peter to be excessive.

2. **Frankness** (v. 28). Peter does not mince matters about the relations of Jews and Gentiles. He gives blunt expression to the facts.

N.B.—This lack of union was due not to the actual law of the Old Testament, but to later accretions through tradition.

3. **Fearlessness** (vv. 28, 29). He tells them without flinching what new lessons God had been teaching him and of his own prompt response.

N.B.—Note here Peter's evident realization of the connection of the *vision* (vv. 11-16) and the *visit* (vv. 17-23): "common or unclean."

4. **Definiteness** (v. 29). Again the real man comes out in this clear-cut request to be told why they wanted him.

N.B.—God had left this to come out gradually as events revealed themselves.

The result was Cornelius' account of his experiences in vv. 30-33.

D. THE APOSTLE'S TESTIMONY
(10:34-43)

1. **His conviction about God's character** (vv. 34, 35). He notes the Divine impartiality and observation of all men. Study the emphasis in Scripture on "respect of persons" (Deut. x. 17; 2 Chron. xix. 7; Luke xx. 21; Rom. ii. 11; Gal. ii. 6; Eph. vi. 9; Jas. ii. 1-9; 1 Pet. i. 17).

2. **His declaration of God's purpose** (vv. 36, 37). A revelation of redemption and peace in Christ.

3. **His revelation of God's love** (vv. 38-41). As seen in Christ's life (v. 38); death (v. 39); resurrection (vv. 40, 41).

4. **His proclamation of God's gospel** (vv. 42, 43). Christ is to be the future Judge; Christ is the present Saviour; remission of sins comes through faith.

E. THE APOSTLE'S JUSTIFICATION
(10:44-48)

It soon became evident that God had been guiding His servant step by step. "The God that answereth by fire" manifested His presence.

1. **The Spirit of God witnessed to the truth** (v. 44). "The Holy Spirit fell" (cf. John xv. 26f.).

2. **The Spirit of God bestowed power** (vv. 45, 46). A second Pentecost.

3. **The Spirit of God warranted discipleship** (v. 47). Baptism was inevitable.

4. **The Spirit of God created fellowship** (v. 48). Peter's stay there strengthened the new-born Church.

F. THE APOSTLE'S DEFENSE (11:1-18)

Tidings soon reached Jerusalem.

1. **Objection was made** (vv. 2, 3). It came from the narrow party within the Church. Note the grounds of objection. It was not against the Gentiles becoming Christian, but against the terms of equality so evident in Peter's fraternization.

2. **Explanation was given** (vv. 4-16). Peter simply narrates the facts in a conciliatory spirit. How unlike the former impulsive, unthinking Peter! (cf. 2 Tim. ii. 24, 25).

3. **Challenge was offered** (v. 17). He throws the *onus* on them. "Who was I that I could withstand God?"

4. **Acknowledgment was made** (v. 18). They accept the explanation and rejoice in the results (cf. "also," vv. 1, 18). Gentiles in the Church.

SUGGESTIONS

1. What Peter learnt

(*a*) **The significance of God's purpose.** In breaking down temporary barriers and bringing in eternal blessings. In extending the Church and thereby realizing his Master's anticipations. John x. 16, "other sheep"; xi. 52, "scattered abroad"; Matt. xxviii. 19, "all nations." The great charter of universal evangelization.

(*b*) **The simplicity of God's plan.** In its *gradual* development of His purpose concerning Gentiles by means of the Samaritans and the Eunuch (viii. 5-38) and in its *natural* development by the simultaneous though separate preparation of **Cornelius** and Peter.

(*c*) **The sufficiency of God's power.** In arranging all circumstances and accomplishing all results. All so simple and natural, and yet all so manifestly Divine.

2. How Peter learnt

(*a*) By keeping his soul close to God (abiding). Note "prayer" in x. 9. Only thus can God reveal His secrets (Ps. xxv. 12, 14). He was spiritually ready.

(*b*) By keeping his mind open to God (attending). Note the "thought" suggested in vv. 17, 19, 28, 34, 47. His intellect realized that the visions and circumstances had a deep meaning.

(*c*) By keeping his will obedient to God (acting). He at once put into practice his new revelations and lessons. To know was to act, and at all costs he carried out his new convictions to their logical and practical outcome.

27

A GREAT DELIVERANCE

THE last important reference to Peter in the Book of the Acts is in connection with the persecution by Herod in Acts xii. 1-17. This was a fresh difficulty for the Church. Already two serious crises had been met: religious persecution at the hands of the Jewish hierarchy (Acts iii., iv.); and Pharisaic narrowness on the part of some of the Jewish Christians (Acts x., xi.) Now comes a conflict with the State, and in connection with it Peter, as one of the leaders, is again brought prominently before us. Study Acts xii.

A. DANGER (Acts 12:1-5)

1. **The prospect** (v. 1). "About that time." Already the trouble of famine (xi. 27-30). "Troubles never come singly." Not a bright outlook for the Church.

2. **The policy** (v. 1). The policy of Herod Agrippa I. was to favor the Jews, and with this object he set himself to persecute the Christians.

3. **The plan** (v. 2). Herod struck at the leaders, thereby intending to deal a mortal blow to the Church. James, the son of Zebedee, was first

killed. He was the first of the Twelve to suffer martyrdom. Remember his request (Mark x. 35-37). It was soon granted. Contrast his brother John's long life of waiting, the last to go (John xxi. 22, 23).

4. **The peril** (v. 3). To please the Jews further, Herod apprehended Peter. After the Passover he too should be killed. Religious scruples alone prevented this murder being committed at once. Here was a significant association of formalism and murderous intent. Formalism is often a cloak of wickedness.

Peter was in charge of sixteen soldiers, probably a guard of four being on duty for one watch each. Note the tribute to Peter's importance and power.

5. **The prayer.** "But prayer" (v. 5). Note the elements of this prayer.

(*a*) Earnest (see R.V.).

(*b*) United, "the church."

(*c*) Definite, "for him."

B. DELIVERANCE (12:6-11)

1. **The peaceful sleep** (v. 6). Note the picture. Within a little of the time proposed by Herod for his death. Contrast Peter's sleep here with the sleep on the Mount of Transfiguration (Luke ix. 32), and the sleep in Gethsemane (Matt. xxvi. 40). Here it was the sleep of perfect trust in God.

2. **The angelic interposition** (vv. 7-9). Note the fulness and vividness of detail.

(*a*) The angel.

(*b*) The light.
(*c*) The action.
(*d*) The words.
(*e*) The results.

3. **The prompt obedience** (vv. 8-10). At each step Peter obeys implicitly and perfectly. Note the difference between his attitude here and in the past.

4. **The Divine limitation** (v. 10). The angel only did for Peter what Peter could not do for himself. Here is a suggestion about the true idea of Divine interpositions and miraculous deliverances.

5. **The full realization** (v. 11). Events had crowded quickly, and he had had no time to realize all that had been done. Now, however, he is himself again, and knows what it all meant. It was "the Lord's doing and marvellous" in his eyes.

C. DELIGHT (12:12-17)

1. **Seeking fellowship** (v. 12). How very characteristic to go where Christians were (cf. Acts iv. 23).

2. **Causing gladness** (vv. 13, 14). How natural and vivid the touches here!

3. **Showing unbelief** (v. 15). It seemed to them utterly impossible.

4. **Expressing astonishment** (v. 16). When he entered they could hardly credit it.

5. **Affording explanation** (v. 17). The glad and wonderful story was soon told. Did they pray for

his preservation and deliverance, and yet did not believe or expect it? Probably not.

(*a*) James had not been spared. Why Peter?

(*b*) Cf. the prayer in Acts iv. 27-30 for possible model of unselfish prayer.

(*c*) Evidently they did not expect to see him again.

(*d*) May they not have prayed for him to be strengthened and enabled to witness a good confession? (cf. v. 5, "for him").

SUGGESTIONS

In this narrative we have illustrated the three greatest powers in the universe.

1. The power of Satan

(*a*) Mighty (vv. 1-4). Causing trouble and suffering. Permission of evil is a great mystery. Therefore *trust and wait*.

(*b*) Limited (vv. 7-10). Satan is not omnipotent or omnipresent. "Thus far shalt thou come." God is still supreme. Therefore *trust and watch*.

(*c*) Doomed (vv. 21-24). Satan's end is certain. Every enemy shall be destroyed. Therefore *trust and work*.

2. The power of God

(*a*) In utter extremity. God is never too late. "Man's extremity is God's opportunity."

(*b*) In apparent impossibility. All appearances were against deliverance. God has many ways of protecting His own.

(*c*) In complete victory. Peter was delivered, the Church reassured, Herod destroyed. "No weapon that is formed against thee shall prosper" (Isa. liv. 17).

3. The power of prayer

(*a*) Possessing God. Prayer links us to Him, and guarantees to us His Divine resource.

(*b*) Overcoming Satan. Linked to God we conquer.

> 'Satan trembles when he sees
> The weakest saint upon his knees.'

(*c*) Blessing man. (1) To Peter prayer brought a quiet conscience, a sense of perfect security and restful hope. (2) To the Church prayer brought comfort in trial, perfecting of character, and a surprise to faith. "Pray, always pray" (Phil, i. 19).

28

PETER AND JOHN

THE allusions in the Gospels and Acts to the associations of Peter with John, the son of Zebedee, afford a striking illustration of the power and blessing of true friendship. Let us consider it now with special reference to Peter, tracing its progress and noting its influence.

A. THEIR EARLY ASSOCIATION

1. **They had similar circumstances** (John i. 41-44; Luke v. 10). They lived at the same place, and their work was not only of the same kind, but was carried on in partnership.

2. **They had common hopes** (John i. 41). Evidently they were both of that earnest company that truly looked forward, with whatever admixture of error, to the coming of the Messiah (Luke ii. 38).

3. **They had characteristic differences.** John was evidently much younger than Peter, and seems to have been the lad among the Apostles. As he was to outlive the others (John xxi. 22), and actually did so for at least from twenty-five to thirty years, we can understand the invariable order of the names of the two brothers "James

and John," and also of "Peter *and John."* John never seems to have taken the initiative in the early days of his discipleship. This youthfulness of John probably accounts for the absence of any jealousy on the part of the other disciples to one who is described as "the disciple whom Jesus loved" and "who leaned on His breast at supper." Contrast the strong feelings evoked at the request of the mother of James and John (Matt. xx. 20-24; Mark x. 35-41).

B. THEIR COMMON DISCIPLESHIP

1. They were *converted* at the same time (John i. 41).

2. They received their *call to definite ministry* at the same time (Luke v. 11).

3. They received their *special Apostolic commission* at the same time (Luke vi. 14; Mark iii. 14-17).

It is in the Gospel of Mark, which is specially associated with Peter, where alone we find the title Boanerges given to James and John.

C. THEIR GROWING FRIENDSHIP

1. Note the *unique privileges* they enjoyed. Three times they were together on very special occasions: "at the raising of Jairus' daughter" (Mark v. 37); "the Transfiguration" (Mark ix. 2); "Gethsemane" (Mark xiv. 33). These occasions not only brought them close to their Master, but also to one another.

2. They were appointed to *special duties* together (Luke xxii. 8). This preparation for the last solemn

Passover was at once an opportunity of united obedience and also of increasing knowledge of their Master and His mission.

3. They were together under *exceptional circumstances*. Here again it is Peter's gospel which gives the detail of this private question of the four disciples (Mark xiii. 3). It is Simon Peter who beckons to John to ask our Lord about the betrayer (John xiii. 24). It is John who uses his influence to bring in Peter to the high priest's palace (John xviii. 15-18). Study also John's account of Peter's fall, and note how gently and simply the story is told.

D. THEIR DEEPENING EXPERIENCES

1. **They journeyed together to the tomb** (John xx. 2-10). Note the vividness of the account; the younger man (John) outruns the older (Peter) and arrives first, yet hesitates to go in. The older man coming up afterwards nevertheless, with characteristic initiative, at once goes in.

2. **They are together on the lake** (John xxi. 7). Contrast the two men here: John is the first to *perceive,* and says, "It is the Lord." Peter is the first to *act,* and at once goes to meet his Lord. A beautiful combination of spiritual perception and eager enthusiasm.

3. **The conversation on the shore** (John xxi. 20-22). Consider Peter's natural interest in his young friend John, in view of our Lord's revelation about his own future.

E. THEIR RIPE FELLOWSHIP

1. **In prayer** (Acts i. 13, iii. 1). Pentecost had taken place with its transforming power, and still the two friends are together in worship of God.

2. **In effort** (Acts iii. 4; Gal. ii. 9). Their service for their Master is still united, and the combination of age and youth, together with their different personal characteristics, make an ideal association for the promotion of their Master's work.

3. **In suffering** (Acts iv. 13, 19, 23). Their testimony was sealed by pain and persecution. They did not flinch before these rulers. Pentecost is still the great explanation of their transformed lives.

SUGGESTIONS

1. **The power of true friendship**

(*a*) *Its cheer.* Companionship is one of the greatest blessings vouchsafed to us by God. "Two are better than one." In all ages Christianity has made much of fellowship and derived much from true friendship.

(*b*) *Its influence.* The union of two diverse temperaments is often the greatest possible blessing to each; one nature becomes the complement of the other. This was especially true of Peter and John. Peter's impulsiveness was balanced by John's caution, while Peter's decision (John xx. 6) counterbalanced John's hesitation (John xx. 5, 8). Peter's ardent zeal was matched and guided by John's spiritual perception. "Peter was a leader, John a lover." "Peter was ready to die for Christ, John to die with Christ."[1]

2. The secret of true friendship

(a) *Its foundation.* Unity in Christ was the basis of the friendship of these men, notwithstanding all other points of contact in early residence and work. Only their oneness in their Lord could have kept them together in fellowship and service for all those years and under all those circumstances.

(b) *Its bonds.* Mutual trust and mutual love are ever the means of genuine fellowship. We see this clearly in the relationship of Peter and John, and the same experiences are always found where true friendship exists.

3. The beautiful variety of Christian discipleship.

No two natures could well be imagined more diverse than those of Peter and John, yet each is a disciple, and each manifests and expresses his discipleship in different ways. There is room for all in the Church of God, and all such diversity illustrates the expression of the Apostle Peter; "The manifold [literally, "variegated"] grace of God" (1 Pet. iv. 10).

---

[1] See W. M. Taylor, D.D., *Peter the Apostle,* pp. 168, 169.

29

PETER AND PAUL

THESE two Apostles in many respects stand out from the rest as the leaders of the early Christian Church. Humanly speaking, earliest Christianity depended more on them than on any of the others. The very structure of the book of the Acts is built up mainly on their lives, chapters i-xii. dealing chiefly with Peter, closing with the account of his imprisonment and release, and chapters xiii.-xxviii. dealing almost exclusively with St. Paul, closing with his imprisonment and (inferred) release. The circumstances of the association of these men are amongst the most interesting and significant incidents of early Church history.

A. THEIR FIRST MEETING (Galatians 1:18)

1. **The time.** Three years after Saul's conversion.

2. **The reason.** "To interview Peter" (Greek). The Apostle of the Gentiles evidently desired to gain information which the Apostle of the circumcision could supply.

3. **The effect.** Paul stayed with Peter fifteen days, and this opportunity of hospitality must have afforded the two men some deeply interesting experiences, each influencing the other and

conveying different impressions of their Master's fellowship.

B. THEIR GREAT CONSULTATION
(2:1-10)

1. **The causes.** During his missionary work in Gentile lands Paul had been experiencing great difficulties with narrow Judaizing Christians. He therefore felt it necessary to confer with the Apostles at Jerusalem on this pressing and serious question.

2. **The circumstances.** Paul went to Jerusalem "by revelation," God thus making known His will to His servant for the unity and furtherance of His work. The consultation took place in private. Probably this visit to Jerusalem is not recorded in the Acts, as there was no need to include it in that historical survey, since it only concerned Paul's personal relation with Jewish Christianity.

3. **The conclusion.** The result was evidently a clear, frank, and hearty recognition of Paul and his sphere of work (v. 9), and thus the matter ended in a way thoroughly satisfactory all round.

C. THEIR SERIOUS DIFFERENCE
(2:11-21)

1. **The time.** Probably this dispute at Antioch took place after the visit of Paul and Barnabas recorded in Acts xi. 30 and xii. 25. Peter's presence at Antioch was possibly a special visit to express appreciation of the famine gift brought by Barnabas and Paul.

2. **The story.** Peter's first attitude on arrival was evidently in entire unison with that of Paul and the Gentile Christians, but the coming of certain Jerusalem Christians led Peter to a change and the adoption of a narrow and really unchristian attitude. This had a profound effect upon other Jewish Christians, and even Barnabas was for the time submerged in this flood of dissimulation. How truly characteristic of Peter was this change of action! The old impulsiveness and timidity reassert themselves, but only for a while.

3. **The result.** Paul quickly saw that this action of Peter and others was not only deplorable on several grounds, but actually wrong, and at once he makes his protest in unmistakable terms. His argument was twofold.

(1) If we Jews cannot keep the law ourselves, why should we compel Gentiles to do what is impossible? (vv. 14-16).

(2) If we Jews left Moses in order to accept Christ, and now return to Moses, we thereby make Christ the minister of sin (vv. 17-21).

D. THEIR STRONG AGREEMENT
(Acts 15)

N.B.—It seems best on every ground to regard the dispute at Antioch as prior to the Council at Jerusalem. It hardly seems possible that Peter could have shown such weakness at Antioch after his pronounced attitude as recorded in Acts xv., while his firm attitude at Jerusalem in the Council would naturally follow after reflection on his mistake at Antioch.[1]

1. **The crisis for Paul**. It was a matter of life and death. Was Christianity to be national or universal, a religion for Jews or for the world, a Jewish sect or a world-wide kingdom?

2. **The action of Peter.** Note how he waited his time (Acts xv. 7) before interposing in the discussion, no longer, as in old days, determined to be first. He is still growing in grace. Dwell upon his appeal to facts within his own and their experience (vv. 7-9). He thereupon shows that the proposal to circumcise Gentiles is at once unnecessary and impossible in the light of God's dealings with Cornelius and his friends (vv. 10, 11). The result of this speech of Peter was unmistakable. The exclusive party could not resist it; and it is evident that in spite of what took place at Antioch, Peter has no real sympathy with the Pharisaic and Judaizing section. In fundamental principles he is entirely one with Paul.

3. **The outcome for Christianity.** The result of the conference was an unmistakable victory for the wider conception of the Gospel laid down by Peter and Paul. Henceforward Christianity is to be without doubt a world-wide religion based on the acceptance of the Lord Jesus Christ through faith.

E. THEIR REAL FELLOWSHIP

1. **Note carefully Paul's attitude to Peter** (1 Cor. i. 12, iii. 21, 22, ix. 5, xv. 5). Paul clearly

[1] See Ramsay's *Galatians* and *St. Paul the Traveller,* and Bartlet's *Apostolic Age.*

acknowledges Peter's prominent and important position as an Apostle of the Lord, working specially among the Jewish Churches.

2. **And Peter's attitude to Paul.** The influence of the greater mind of Paul is evident all through Peter's First Epistle. A careful comparison of Romans and Ephesians with 1 Peter will reveal this to all students (cf., *e.g.,* Gal. v. 13 and 1 Pet. ii. 16). Peter's reference to Paul in 2 Pet. iii. 15, 16 is as significant as it is hearty. Paul is "our beloved brother," and his Epistles are placed on a level with "the other Scriptures." The assimilative temperament of Peter could not but imbibe Pauline teaching.

3. **And the links between them.** Two men were associated both with Paul and Peter, and a consideration of these two disciples helps us to understand the true relationship of the two Apostles. As to Mark, cf. Col. iv. 10; 2 Tim. iv. 11; 1 Pet. v. 13. As to Silas, cf. 2 Cor. i. 19; 1 Pet. v. 12.

SUGGESTIONS

1. **Unity in variety, and variety in unity.** How different were these two men in social circumstances, natural temperament, intellectual power, and spiritual opportunity! Yet there is room for both and need of both; and, however different they are essentially one in Christ. He it is Who reconciles all differences and provides for the use of the most diverse powers in His kingdom.

2. **Expediency versus principle.** Peter's weakness at Antioch illustrates the danger of expediency when principle is involved. There are

times when expediency may guide action, but never at the cost of principle. Paul's unflinching stand on principle, however severe it may have seemed at the time, was vital to the continuance of true Christianity in the young Church at Antioch.

3. **The ultimate tendencies of timidity and courage.** Timidity, if allowed to go to extremes, will result in weakness. Courage, if pressed exclusively, may lead to undue sternness. Herein we see the need of balance in Christian life and character, timidity being safeguarded by courage, and courage being actuated and guided by discretion and love.

4. **Differences between Christians.** In the dispute between Peter and Paul we have the two great secrets whereby differences may be resolved. (1) They should be *faced squarely,* as Paul felt led to do, for there is no use whatever in ignoring differences where vital principles are involved. At the same time (2) they should be *met lovingly,* as Peter undoubtedly did. Nothing can be more delightful to contemplate than the entire absence of any resentment on the part of Peter or any trace of personal feeling afterwards, as the result of the dispute. He evidently realized his error, and accepted the situation in the true spirit of Christ. In the light of former outbursts of temper before Pentecost we can see here Peter's striking growth in grace.

30

SPIRITUAL MATURITY

In order to have a complete view of the Apostle's character it is necessary to study the Epistles for their personal revelation of his mature Christian life and experience. We thus reach the summit of his career and see the culmination of the process whereby "Simon" was transformed into "Peter." We can give but the merest fragment of the entire subject, and the following outline is intended only as the framework of further and fuller study. Let us note three aspects of Peter's (and indeed every) true, growing, ripening Christian life.

A. DOCTRINAL KNOWLEDGE

1. Concerning God
The Trinity (1 Pet. i. 2).
Father (1 Pet. i. 3, 17).
Creator (1 Pet. iv. 19; 2 Pet. iii. 5-7).
2. Concerning our Lord
Son (1 Pet. i. 3).
Redeemer (1 Pet. i. 19, ii. 24; 2 Pet. i. 1, 11, ii.20.)
God (1 Pet. i. 20; 2 Pet. i. 1, 16).
Example (1 Pet. ii. 21).
Sufferings (1 Pet. iv. 1, 13, v. 1).

Resurrection (1 Pet. i. 3, 21, iii. 21).
Lordship (2 Pet. ii. 1).

3. Concerning the Holy Spirit
Sanctification (1 Pet. i. 2).
Inspiration (1 Pet. i. 11f.; 2 Pet. i. 21).
Purification (1 Pet. i. 22).

4. Concerning Scripture
Its inspiration (1 Pet. i. 10-12; 2 Pet. i. 21).
Its contents: (1) Quotations (1 Pet. i. 24, ii. 3-10). (2) Allusions (1 Pet. iii. 6, 20, v. 5, 7; 2 Pet. ii. 4-7, 15).

5. Concerning the Christian life
Election (1 Pet. i. 2).
Regeneration (1 Pet. i. 3).
Forgiveness (2 Pet. i. 9).
Sanctification (1 Pet. i. 2; 2 Pet. i. 4-8).
Joy (1 Pet. i. 6, 8).
Separation (1 Pet. i. 1, ii. 11).
Obedience (1 Pet. i. 2, 14).
Future salvation (1 Pet. i. 5).
Knowledge (2 Pet. i. 2, 3, iii. 18).
Growth (2 Pet. i. 5, 11, iii. 18).

6. Concerning the Church
The spiritual Israel (1 Pet. ii. 5-10).
The spiritual brotherhood (1 Pet. ii. 17, v. 9).
The Christian ministry (1 Pet. v. 1 ff.).
The general service (1 Pet. iv. 10f.).

7. Concerning the future life
The last days (1 Pet. iv. 7: 2 Pet. iii. 3).
Death (2 Pet. i. 13-15).
Judgment (1 Pet. i. 17, ii. 23, iv. 5).

The Lord's coming (1 Pet. i. 7, 13, v. 4; 2 Pet. iii. 10, 12).
Glory (1 Pet. i. 11, 21, iv. 13, v. 10).
Heaven (1 Pet. i. 4, 5; 2 Pet. iii. 13).

B. SPIRITUAL EXPERIENCE

1. Faith
Its object (1 Pet. i. 8).
Its warrant (1 Pet. i. 21).
Its value (2 Pet. i. 1).

2. Love
To God (1 Pet. i. 8).
To Christians (1 Pet. i. 22).
To the world (1 Pet. ii. 17; 2 Pet. i. 7).

3. Hope
Its expectation—Glory (1 Pet. i. 3, 13).
Its foundation—God (1 Pet. i. 21).
Its test—Trial (1 Pet. i. 7, iii. 15).

b. Holiness
Its source (1 Pet. i. 2).
Its progress (2 Pet. i. 5-7).
Its manifestation (2 Pet. i. 4-8).

5. Fear
Its need (1 Pet. i. 17, ii. 17).
Its character (1 Pet. ii. 18, iii. 2, 15).
Its contrast (1 Pet. iii. 6, 14).

6. Joy
Its foundation—God (1 Pet. i. 6, 8, iv. 13).
Its secret—Experience (1 Pet. i. 8).
Its power—Certitude (1 Pet. i. 8; 2 Pet. i. 2).

7. Consistency

Its emphasis—"Well-doing" (see Part II., Study 29).

Its expression—Life (1 Pet. ii. 11, iii. 16; 2 Pet. i. 5-10).

Its extent—Everything (2 Pet. iii. 11. See Part II., Study 29).

C. PERSONAL CHARACTER

1. Old excellences confirmed

Courage (John xviii. 10; 1 Pet. iii. 15, iv. 13).
Energy (John xxi. 3; 1 Pet. v. 8, 9).
Zeal (Matt. xiv. 28; 1 Pet. i. 13, 22).
Promptness (John xx. 4; 2 Pet. i. 10).

2. Old deficiencies supplied

Steadfastness (1 Pet. v. 10; 2 Pet. i. 10, 12; iii. 16, 17).
Humility (1 Pet. v. 6, 7).
Tenderness (1 Pet. ii. 11, iv. 12, v. 1; 2 Pet. i. 1, i. 12, iii. 1, 14).

3. Old tendencies transformed

Self-satisfaction (Matt. xvii. 4) into meekness (1 Pet. iii. 15).

Selfishness ("What shall we have?"—Matt. xix. 27) into unselfishness ("Such as I have, give I," Acts iii. 6).

Presumption (Matt. xiv. 28) into godly fear (1 Pet. i. 17).

Thoughtlessness (Matt. xvi. 22) into spiritual experience (1 Pet. v. 6, 7).

Impulsiveness (John xiii. 37) into well-directed enthusiasm (1 Pet. ii. 12, iii. 16).

4. Old lessons remembered
About faith (John xx. 29; 1 Pet. i. 8).
About humility (John xiii. 4-8; 1 Pet. v. 5).
About death (John xxi. 18, 19; 2 Pet. i. 14).
About watchfulness (Luke xii. 35; 1 Pet. i. 13).
About service (John xxi. 15f.; I Pet. v. 2).

SUGGESTIONS

1. **The conquests of grace.** What it does for us.
(*a*) The transformation in the Apostle.
(*b*) The sole explanation—Divine grace.

2. **The course of grace.** How it works in us.
(*a*) Reception of Divine truth.
(*b*) Truth transmuted into experience.
(*c*) Experience forming habit.
(*d*) Habit settling into character.
(*e*) Character tending increasing to permanence.

3. **The conditions of grace.** What it requires from us.
(*a*) Faith in the power of God.
(*b*) Feeding on the Word of God.
(*c*) Fulness of the Spirit of God.
(*d*) Fellowship with the Son of God.
(*e*) Faithfulness to the will of God.

Part 2

The Epistles

31

INTRODUCTION TO THE
FIRST EPISTLE

AFTER studying the character and work of the Apostle of the Circumcision, we naturally turn to the consideration of his writings. The letters shed light on the life of the writer, and enable us to see him as he was in his later days, some twelve years (perhaps) after the last record we have of him in Acts (chap. xv.), or (perhaps) six years after his difference with St. Paul (Gal. ii.). Grace had been silently but really continuing its work in deepening and maturing Peter's experience, and the result is what we find in these two Epistles.

But beyond all this, the human and personal side, the Epistles are a valuable and important contribution to the sum total of the truth revealed in the New Testament, and as such they specially call for our careful and prayerful study.

PRELIMINARY CONSIDERATIONS

It is both necessary and helpful, in taking up a new work, to seek to discover all we can about the author and circumstances of the composition. To these inquiries we must now address ourselves.

1. **The author.** By whom was it written? Two or three personal allusions answer this question. He calls himself "Peter, an apostle of Jesus Christ" (i. 1); "a fellow elder, and a witness of the sufferings of Christ" (v. 1). This internal testimony is endorsed by the consensus of Christian tradition through the centuries as to the Petrine authorship of this Epistle.

2. **The destination.** To whom was it written? It is addressed to Christians in five divisions of the Roman Empire (i. 1) which answer generally to Asia Minor as we now know it. It is evident from these names that there were other Churches in Asia Minor than those founded by St. Paul and his disciples, as recorded in the Acts and Pauline Epistles (see allusion to spread of Christianity in Col. i. 6).

3. **The purpose.** Why was it written? The answer to this is found in chap. v. 12. The purpose is twofold—

(*a*) Encouragement, "exhorting." It is eminently an Epistle of exhortation. The Greek word used here is equivalent to the title of the Holy Spirit, "Paraclete," "The Comforter" (John xiv.), and means much more than our modern idea of "Consolation." "Comfort" really includes three thoughts: (1) Making *strong* (cf. *fortress*). (2) Making *brave* (cf. *fortitude*). (3) Making *happy, i.e.* the modern meaning of comfort. Read the Epistle through, and note how this threefold idea runs through the whole teaching.

(*b*) Assurance, "testifying." The word implies strong or earnest personal witness," and is a natural

outcome of the former idea of exhortation. The
Apostle adds his own personal assurance to what he
writes, as though to say, "I can endorse all I say
from my own experience." Read through the Epistle
again, and note this personal aspect underlying all.
The testimony thus given is to "the true grace of
God," in which he urges his readers to continue to
stand (R.V.).

4. **The reason.** Why was it written? The above
purpose had a *reason* behind it. Certain circumstances led to this letter of exhortation and testimony. The Christians to whom the Apostle wrote
were experiencing a time of trial (i. 6, iii. 14, iv. 12,
16), and hence the need of "encouragement" and
personal "witness" from an Apostle of Christ, and
one who knew what trial meant. This encouragement takes a threefold form. He bids them think
(1) of the future glory (i. 7), (2) of the example of
Christ (ii. 21), and (3) of the reward which will
follow suffering (iv. 13, v. 1, 6).

5. **The date.** When was it written? The reference to duty to the State (ii. 13-17), together with
allusions to Silvanus (Silas) and Mark (v. 12,
13), have suggested (with great probability) that
this Epistle was written from Rome (Babylon,
cf. Rev. xvii., xviii.) soon after the release of St.
Paul (Phil. i. 25; Philem. 22). Thus the fact of
St. Peter writing to Churches some of which
were associated with St. Paul, and sending the
letter by one of St. Paul's companions, would be
a beautiful and helpful testimony to the essential
unity of the two great Apostles working together
for their Master.

6. **The characteristics.** With what features was it written.

(*a*) Clearly influenced deeply by the Old Testament, especially in its Greek version (LXX. or Septuagint). Note quotations and allusions.

(*b*) Evident allusions also to St. Paul's Epistles, especially Romans and Ephesians (cf. i. 21 with Rom. iv. 20, 24, 25; ii. 8-10 with Rom. ix.; ii. 6, 7 with ix. 33).

(*c*) Manifest connection with the Epistle of St. James (cf. i. 1 of each Epistle; Jas. i. 2, 3 and 1 Pet. i. 6f.; Jas. iv. 6, 7, 10; and 1 Pet. v. 5-9).

(*d*) The Greek of the Epistle shows that the writer had an "easy mastery" over the language. If this is surprising in a Galilean, may it not be accounted for by regarding the Epistle as Peter's thoughts clothed in the language of Silvanus, as the amanuensis of the Apostle? (cf. Rom. xvi. 22).

ANALYSIS OF THE EPISTLE

It is not systematic or logical in arrangement, simply because it consists largely of exhortations based on the spiritual needs of the readers. The main breaks seem to be at ii. 11 and iv. 12, thus offering—

1. **A short conspectus**

(*a*) i. 1—ii. 10: Privileges.
(*b*) ii. 11—iv. 11: Duties.
(*c*) iv. 12—v. 14: Trials.

(See *Hastings' Bible Dictionary,* A r t i c l e, "Peter"). These three sections can only be approximately distinct, for the topics overlap in the various parts. Yet it will prove useful to read through the Epistle and not these main ideas of each section.

N.B.—Nothing can compare with reading an Epistle through at once, and reading it, if possible, twice or thrice over at one time. Then the way becomes clear for

2. A longer analysis

(*a*) Opening salutations (i 1, 2).

(*b*) Thanksgiving, introducing the main thoughts of the Epistle—grace, suffering, glory (i. 3-12).

(*c*) General exhortations in view of the present (i. 13—ii. 10).

(*d*) Special exhortations as to sufferings and glory (ii. 11—iv. 6).

(*e*) General exhortations in view of the end (iv. 7-19).

(*f*) Special exhortations as to sufferings and glory (v. 1-9).

(*g*) Prayer, summarizing the main thoughts of the Epistle—grace, suffering, glory (v. 10, 11).

(*h*) Closing salutations (v. 12-14).

N.B.—It will be seen that the longer analysis (based on Dr. Bullinger's outline) differs from the shorter in making one section end with iv. 6 instead of iv. 11. Dr. Hort, in his valuable work on this Epistle, notes that ii. 11 and iv. 12 begin with "Beloved," thus seeming to mark a new section. He thinks that iv. 7-11 are rather a close to what precedes than an introduction to what follows, though also partly transitional.

More detailed analysis will be shown in each section as we proceed.

32

DIVINE GRACE
(1 Peter 1:1-5)

THE careful and minute study of this Epistle sheds much light on the character and experience of the Apostle, and also brings before us several aspects of inspired teaching. It is very important to compare the A.V. and R.V. The latter is a great help in many passages.

THE SALUTATION
(1:1-2)

1. **The writer**

(*a*) His name: "Peter." The old name "Simon" was early disused, though found in 2 Pet. i. 1 (see first Study in Part I.).

(*b*) His office: "Apostle of Jesus Christ." Title combines ideas of *authority* and *ability,* and *warrant* for writing (cf. 1 Cor. ix. 1). Study uses of term "apostle" in New Testament. First applied to "the Twelve"; then wider application, almost meaning "missionary" (Acts xiv. 4; 2 Cor. viii. 23, Greek; Rom. xvi. 7). Dwell on the Apostleship of Peter as a miracle and marvel of Divine grace.

2. **The readers.** Note the threefold description

(*a*) The temporariness of their abode. R.V., "sojourners" (cf. i. 17, ii. 11; Heb. xi. 13). "Here we have no continuing city" (Heb. xiii. 14). "God hath prepared for them a city" (Heb. xi. 16).

(*b*) The solitariness of their condition. R.V., "dispersion" (cf. John vii. 35 and Acts ii. 5 for literal Jewish dispersion). Here it is also spiritual, and includes all Christians (cf. ii. 11), "strangers and pilgrims" (cf. Jas. i. 1, R.V.).

(*c*) The glory of their privilege: "Elect."

(1) The *nature* of election: "Elect." Scripture teaches election under various aspects. (*a*) To opportunity, *ie.* of hearing the Gospel. Contrast Britain and Tibet. (*b*) To privilege, *i.e.* of present possession of Gospel (John xv. 16-19). (*c*) To service, *i.e.* to special work for God (Luke vi. 13; Acts ix. 15; 1 Pet. ii. 9). (*d*) To salvation (Eph. i. 4; 1 Thess. i. 4). On this last point note carefully that Scripture emphasizes the two sides of salvation, God's and man's, sometimes one and sometimes the other, but never attempts to reconcile them. They are like parallel lines, both necessary, both important, but never meeting this side of eternity. Our wisdom is to follow Scripture, and lay stress on both parts of God's salvation. Grace prompts it, grace provides it, perfects it. But grace works through human means and conditions. Note the perfect balance of both sides in these passages (John x. 27, 28; Rom. viii. 29, 30; 2 Thess. ii. 13; 2 Tim. ii. 19; 1 Pet. i. 2; Jude 21).

(2) The *source* of election: "According to the foreknowledge of God the Father." This is the Divine standard or rule. Foreknowledge in God means more than foresight of human actions (cf. Jer. i. 5; Acts. ii. 23; Rom. viii. 29 and xi. 2; 1 Pet.

i. 20; 2 Pet. iii. 17). It means foresight and definite knowledge of His own Divine plan and purpose. It is something more than foresight and something less than fore-ordination.

(3) The *sphere* of election: "In sanctification of the Spirit." This is how the election realizes itself in the life of the believer. It is by the Spirit (cf. 2 Thess. ii. 13). "Sanctification" primarily means separation, hallowing, consecration, and this is by or "in" the Holy Spirit. The Holy Spirit works in the new-born soul and *sets it apart* for God.

(4) The *purpose* of election: "Unto obedience and sprinkling of the blood of Jesus Christ." This is the twofold outcome of the work of grace. (*a*) Obedience, *i.e.* true Christian loyalty to Christ (cf. i. 22). (*b*) Sprinkling, *i.e.* the personal application and appropriation of the atoning Sacrifice, whereby our lives enter into and abide in covenant with God. Distinguish the "sprinkling" from the *shedding* of the sacrificial blood (cf. Exod. xxiv. 3-8; Heb. ix. 7-22, x. 22, xii. 24). Thus the crowning purpose of God's election is the life in covenant with God and experienced in obedience. Sprinkling is the Divine act of marking our entrance into covenant with God through the blood.

3. **The prayer:** "Grace to you, and peace, be multiplied."

(*a*) Grace. The Divine gift. "Force" would be a good modern equivalent. "God's favor expressed in a gift of power." Study use in New Testament. It is the word used in Greek salutations.

(*b*) "Peace." The human result. Includes reconciliation and rest. The Hebrew salutation.

(*c*) "Grace and peace." Cause and effect. Active and passive sides. The Gospel combines the Greek and Hebrew needs in its universality of provision.

(*d*) "Multiplied." Over and over again the same great need and same abundant supply (cf. Hebrew benediction in Num. vi. 24-26). After opening salutation comes a burst of praise (cf. Eph. i. 1-3).

SPECIAL NOTES FOR FURTHER STUDY

(1) **The Trinity here.** Contrast Paul's salutation with Father and Son only. Note order here: Father, Spirit, Son. Compare 2 Cor. xiii. 14: "Son, Father, Spirit"—John xiv. 16: "Son, Father, Spirit"—John xiv. 26: "Spirit, Father, Son"—John xv. 26: "Spirit, Son, Father"—1 Cor. xii. 4-6: "Spirit, Son, Father."

(2) Note the *three prepositions*: "According to," "in," "unto." Standard, sphere, and purpose.

(3) The *amplification* of the idea of "foreknowledge of the Father" in vv. 3-12; of the "sanctification of the Spirit" in vv. 13-17; of obedience and sprinkling in vv. 18-25.

PRAISE (1:3:5)

1. **The Object of praise**

(*a*) God in Himself. "God and Father." Note combination of Deity and Fatherhood. One balances the other.

(*b*) God in relation to Christ. "God of." "Father of" (cf. John xx. 17; Eph. i. 3, 17). An attempt to express the profound but mysterious truth of the "subordination" of the Eternal Son of God.

(*c*) God in relation to us. *"Our* Lord Jesus Christ." Note the three titles, Lord, Jesus, Christ. See them separately in Acts ii. 36, and *first* brought together in Acts xi. 17.

2. The reasons for praise

(*a*) The present experience: "Begotten" (John iii. 5; 1 Pet. i. 23).

(*b*) The future prospect. Threefold, "unto."

(1) "Unto a living hope" (cf. Prov. xi. 7, xiv. 32; Titus ii. 13; 1 John iii. 2, 3).

(2) "Unto an inheritance." New Testament idea of inheritance includes possession as well as expectation (cf. Gen. xv. 7, 8; Eph. i. 18. Note four characteristics: "Uncorrupt," "unpolluted," "unwithered," "reserved in heaven for you, who are kept by the power of God through faith," *i.e.* stability, purity, beauty, certainty.

N.B.—Mark the balance of truth here: "Kept," "for," "by," and "through."

(3) "Unto salvation." Salvation has three characteristics: past, present, future. It includes deliverance from sin's penalty, power, and presence (cf. Acts xvi. 30; Acts ii. 47, Greek; 1 Cor. xv. 2, Greek; Rom. v. 9, 10, viii. 24; Heb. i. 14, vii. 25, ix. 28; 1 Pet. i. 9, ii. 22, iv. 18). This future salvation is even now "ready," but not yet "revealed." It will be "in the last time," "when things are at their worst" (HORT) (cf. 1 John ii. 18; Jude 18), or "when the Lord comes" (John vi. 40).

(*c*) The sure guarantee: "By the resurrection" (cf. Rom. i. 4, iv. 25; 1 Cor. xv. *passim;* Eph. ii. 6, 7; John xiv. 19).

(*d*) The wonderful explanation: "According to His great mercy" (v. 3). This alone is the source of all God's provision of grace (1 John iii. 1; Eph. ii. 4).

3. The power of praise

"Blessed be God," literally "speak well of God" (cf. Ps. c. 3, "Speak good of His Name"—Prayer Book version). Why should we? Because—

1. Praise is the expression of gratitude. We realize, "Oh, to grace how great a debtor!"

2. Praise is the expression of humility. It enables us to say, "Not unto us, O Lord, but unto Thy Name give glory" (Ps. cxv. 1).

3. Praise is the expression of confession: "Let the redeemed of the Lord *say so*" (Ps. cvii. 1, 2; Ps. xxxiv. 1-2).

4. Praise is the expression of satisfaction: "Satisfied with favor, full with the blessing of the Lord (Deut. xxxiii. 23). We rejoice and exalt in the perfect provision of abounding grace (Ps. cvii. 8, 9, "for.")

33

SALVATION
(1 Peter 1:6-12)

THE keynote of the whole section (vv. 3-12) is "Salvation," a word which occurs three times (vv. 5, 9, 10). Note, as already suggested, the amplification of the ideas connected with "elect according to the foreknowledge of God the Father" (v. 2).

A. SALVATION: ITS PRECIOUSNESS AND POWER (1:6-9)

After dwelling on the future glories of God's grace, the Apostle turns to notice its power over the believer's present life.

1. **The experience of joy** (v. 6)

(*a*) The explanation of joy. "Wherein," *i.e.* "in which" circumstances of new life and hopes recorded in vv. 3-5. This is the reason why joy is possible.

(*b*) The expression of joy, "rejoice" (literally, "*exult*"). Two words in New Testament Greek are rendered "joy." (1) The constant state or normal *experience* of joy. (2) The active, *energetic expression* of joy. Here it is the latter. It denotes the vigor and force of joyous exultation in the Gospel.

2. The experience of sorrow (v. 6)

This experience exists side by side with the former, and is one of the Christian paradoxes, the co-existence of joy and sorrow in the believer. How is this possible? See what follows:

(*a*) The cause. "Temptations," *i.e.* trials; not incitements to evil, but causes of suffering (cf. Gen. xxii. 1, "test"). Note here that trials were the outward circumstances of their life, while their joy was the underlying foundation. Distinguish carefully between happiness and joy. Happiness depends on what *happens,* is connected with the "happenings" of life, with circumstances. Joy is underneath and independent of circumstances, and is a condition of soul in relation to the Lord. Hence it is possible to be joyful within, even when circumstances are untoward and difficult. We can be joyful even when through circumstances we are "unhappy" (cf. 2 Cor. vi. 10, "sorrowful," *i.e.* not "happy," *yet alway rejoicing*). Hence the paradox as above. Let us live in that which is deepest and permanent, and this will enable us to meet all circumstances.

(*b*) The character: "Manifold." No two experiences alike. Varied trials in life.

(*c*) The necessity: "If needs be." Always a "needs be" for trial, even if God's reason is not always at once known.

(*d*) The duration: "A time." "Just now for a little while." The limitation is certain. "God holds the key" (2 Cor. iv. 17, 18).

3. The purpose of sorrow (v. 7). Note three stages:

(*a*) The testing of faith. Why *faith?* Why not love, hope, patience? Because faith is the foundation of all. If that goes, all goes. If that stands, all will stand. Note the comparison of faith and gold. Gold is tested by fire; faith is tested by trial.

(*b*) The proving of faith. Testing metal at once cleanses and proves it. So with trial of faith. It purifies and strengthens while it proves. Note the further comparison of faith and gold: "More precious." Gold is a *pure* metal, *solid, ductile, valuable.* So is faith spiritually.

N.B.—The Greek suggests that the *proof* as well as the *faith* is to be included in the comparison (cf. Jas. i. 3). We could render, "The proved residue of your faith."

(*c*) The approving of faith. "Might be found unto praise and honor and glory at the revelation of Jesus Christ." Proof leads to approval. Note these three words, "Praise, glory, honor," *i.e.* acknowledgment in *word* (praise); in *deed* (glory); in *feeling* (honor). God's praise of us. God's glory in us. God's value of us (cf. Rom. ii. 7, 10; 1 Cor. iv. 5). This is to take place at the "unveiling of Jesus Christ." All the direct future for believers is concentrated in that day.

4. **The power of joy** (vv. 8, 9)

Again the Apostle turns to the joy of the Gospel.

(*a*) The characteristics of joy.

(1) "Unspeakable," *i.e.* cannot be expressed, ineffable, unutterable. So always with the deepest experiences.

(2) "Full of glory" (literally, "glorified"), *i.e.* already marked with the splendor of heaven. Heaven anticipated now.

N.B.—Some writers think this description too high for present experiences; but the whole context clearly refers to present, and not future. Probably our average low experience tends to make us doubt the possibilities of present joy.

(*b*) The channels of joy. How does it come?

(1) *Through love*: "Whom not having seen, ye love." "Unseen, but not unknown." Another Christian paradox: love for an unseen Master.

(2) *Through faith*: "In Whom, though now we see Him not, yet believing" (cf. John xx. 29). Faith is a spring of joy, because it makes Christ real.

(3) *Through hope*: "Receiving the end of your faith, even the salvation of your souls." "Receiving" here implies obtaining and appropriating, acquiring and making our own. "The end," *i.e.* the completion and crown, the end and aim of all trust. So we look forward, and hope brings joy. Let us therefore live "beneath the surface," below circumstances, and "dwell deep" in the joy of the Lord through faith, love, and hope. A Christian is never to be "under the circumstances," but *above* them, by means of joy in the Lord.

B. SALVATION: ITS GREATNESS AND GLORY (1:10-12)

Note connection between this and the foregoing section. A salvation now to be considered in its greatness and glory (vv. 10-12) can surely be depended on to uphold us in present trials (vv. 7-9). Wherein is its greatness and glory? In being the subject of deep interest on every hand.

1. **The subject of prophetic study** (vv. 10, 11)

(*a*) The prophets' work was to predict the coming of grace, "who prophesied of the grace that should come unto you."

(*b*) The prophets themselves were deeply interested in their own prophecies, "sought and searched" (v. 10). They wished to know the *time* and *circumstances* of the Messiah's coming (v. 11).

(*c*) The prophets' message was summed up in the "sufferings and glory" of the Messiah (v. 11; cf. Luke xxiv. 26; Heb. ii. 9). (1) For suffering (cf. Isa. liii.) (2) For glory (cf. Isa. ix., xi.).

(*d*) The prophets were instructed that their predictions were not for themselves (alone), but for the future (v. 12; cf. Heb. xi. 13, 39, 40).

N.B.—Collect the ten references in 1 Peter to the title of "Christ" (without "Jesus" or "Lord"), a somewhat unusual title.

2. **The subject of Apostolic testimony** (v. 12)

(*a*) The message: "Gospel."

(*b*) The messengers: "Them that preached."

(*c*) The method: "Announced."

(*d*) The might: "By the Holy Ghost."

3. **The subject of Divine inspiration**

(*a*) The Spirit of Christ in the prophets of the Old Testament (v. 11).

(*b*) The Holy Ghost in the preachers of the New Testament (v. 12).

4. **The subject of angelic inquiry** (v. 12)

(*a*) Their earnestness: "Desire."

(*b*) Their eagerness: "Look into" (cf. John xx. 5-11, Greek). The angels are not superior, but inferior to believers in point of position, privilege, knowledge (Eph. iii. 10; 1 Cor. vi. 3; Heb. i. 14).

5. **The subject of human reception** (v. 12)

Note "unto you" (v. 10); "unto us" (v. 12); "unto you" (v. 12). This salvation was intended for us, for our reception and use. Hence the five-fold glory of this salvation. It is the central topic of the universe, occupying the attention of God, prophets, apostles, believers, and angels.

SPECIAL STUDIES

1. **Consider the Apostle's view of the Old Testament**

(*a*) As a book containing a definite predictive element.

(*b*) As a book manifestly inspired by the Spirit of God.

Contrast this with certain modern views of the Old Testament. We cannot go far wrong if we abide by the Apostle's testimony.

2. **Mark the essential unity between the Old and New Testaments**

(*a*) The one looks forward (vv. 10, 11); the other backward (v. 12), "now."

(*b*) Both are inspired by the one Spirit of God (vv. 10, 12).

3. **Note the inspired summary of what constitutes the Gospel**

(*a*) The sufferings of Christ, *i.e.* death.

(*b*) The glory of Christ, *i.e.* Resurrection, Ascension, and Pentecost (v. 12): "sent down from heaven."

CONCLUSION

Review vv. 3-12, and note the connection of thought.

(*a*) 3-5: Praise to God for present and future salvation.

(*b*) 6-9: This salvation causes joy even in the midst of sorrows.

(*c*) 10-12: Its greatness and glory seen in the universal interest it excites.

34

HOPE
(1 Peter 1:13-16)

HITHERTO (vv. 3-12) we have been concerned with certain aspects of the *fact* of salvation; its joy (vv. 3-5), its power (vv. 6-9), its glory (vv. 10-12). Now we consider certain *fruits* of salvation. The first of these is HOPE. A careful study of the R.V. and Greek shows that "hope" is the principal subject of v. 13, and that the other topics are subsidiary.

A. THE CALL TO HOPE (1:13)

1. **The meaning of hope** (cf. v. 3, "living hope"). Our modern ideas and expressions of "hope" and "hopefulness" are vague, indefinite, and often of little use. In the New Testament hope is a definite grace of the Holy Spirit, and has unmistakable practical power. It may perhaps be defined as "the Christian attitude of the soul in relation to the future." Contrast and compare it with faith. Faith is concerned with the Person of Christ, hope with the things of Christ. Faith fixes itself on the promiser, hope on the thing promised. Faith looks upward, hope looks forward. Faith accepts, hope expects. Faith appropriates, hope anticipates. Hope therefore is

occupied with the future, and centers itself on that which is coming. Its immediate expectation is "the revelation of Jesus Christ" (vv. 7, 13).

2. **The duty of hope.** We can now see that hope is a *duty,* a positive command. It is so because it is (in the New Testament sense) not a matter of emotions, but of the will. It calls for obedience.

3. **The power of hope** (see R.V., "Hope perfectly"; A.V., "to the end," is inadequate). The idea is rather of the perfection than the persistence of hope, though the latter is included. A perfect hope must be marked by: (1) Certainty, (2) Continuity. The certainty must be due to adequate warrant or basis (as in vv. 3-12). The continuity must be our constant response to this well-grounded hope.

B. THE SUBSTANCE OF HOPE (1:13)

1. **What** are we expecting? "Grace." The term as here used is equivalent to what has been described in v. 3, "living hope"; v. 4, "inheritance"; v. 5, "salvation"; v. 7, "revelation"; v. 9, "end of faith." It is another word for that glory or complete salvation which will be ours hereafter.

N.B.—1. Authors differ as to whether "grace" here is the "object" of hope (that for which we hope) or the "ground" of hope (that because of which we hope). Probably both ideas are to be included.

N.B.—2. Study carefully the meaning of "grace." (1) Originally a characteristic of *beauty* (cf. our "grace" of manner). (2) Next, an attitude of *favor*.

(3) Then, the specifically Christian meaning, a gift of *force*. (4) Lastly, as the outcome, an expression of *thanks* (cf. our saying "Grace"). Study the Greek word *charis* and its cognates in the New Testament under the above aspects.

2. **How** are we expecting? "Is to be brought unto you" (literally, "is being brought'). Grace is already on its way. It is continually coming. It has been coming through the centuries, and will one day culminate.

3. **When** are we expecting? "At the revelation of Jesus Christ." The future day of the "unveiling" of our Lord (cf. Gal. i. 16 for present spiritual unveilings). All our hope is centered on "that blessed hope."

C. THE WARRANT OF HOPE (1:13)

1. **Its Divine basis.** Note force of "wherefore." Refers back to vv. 3-12. The foundation of our hope is God's revelation in Christ with all its promises for the future. This offers and assures us of that certainty which is a necessary element of a "perfect" hope. Dwell much on these foundations of hope.

2. **Its practical power.** Intended to influence us in daily living (cf. "sanctification," v. 2). The attitude of hope has two elements, desire and expectation. We may desire and not expect, and we may expect and not desire. Neither of these is hope. Contrast the hope of the hypocrite (Job viii. 13) and of the self-deceived. The Christian hope lasts because it is in God (v. 21). As Leigh-

ton says, not only can the Christian say, *"Dum spiro, spero"* ("While I breathe, I hope"), but *"Dum ex-spiro, spero"* ("While I am breathing my last, I hope).

D. THE SUPPORTS OF HOPE (1:13)

Hope needs to be supported and guided, and here we have two such sources of strength.

1. **Concentration of purpose:** "Girding up the loins of your mind" (cf. Exod. xii. 11; 1 Kings xviii. 46; Luke xii. 35, 46; John xiii. 4-16; Eph. vi. 14). The figure suggests the fastening up of the flowing Eastern robes, so as not to impede progress. Preparation for work. Promptitude, not slackness. "Pull yourself together." Note the referenec to "mind": why not "heart"? Emphasis on intellectual faculties as the source of power. Vigorous thought leads to vigorous action, feeble thought to feeble action (cf. Matt. xxii. 37, "thy mind," 2 Pet. iii. 1). "The moral discipline of thought and reason" (HORT). No dissipation of mental and moral powers, but definite, energetic concentration.

2. **Control of powers:** "Be sober" (cf. 1 Pet. iv. 7 and v. 8; 1 Thess. v. 6-8; 2 Tim. iv. 5). Primary reference to drunkenness, and then wider reference to stupefactions of all kinds. No excitements, no indulgences; powers well in hand and fully awake .

N.B.—1. Note how these support and strengthen hope, enabling the soul to concentrate itself on future without distraction of thought or dissipation of energy.

N.B.—2. Some authorities connect the adverb "perfectly" with "be sober," instead of with "hope." "Be perfectly sober, and hope." Hort quotes i. 22, ii. 19, ii. 23 in support of the adverb coming after (and not before) its verb (in the Greek). But we prefer to follow those who, with the R. V., keep the older association.

E. THE REASONS FOR HOPE (1:14-16)

The connection of these verses with the foregoing is variously given. Some commence a new paragraph dealing with holiness. But it seems best to connect hope and holiness, and regard these verses as a continuation and amplification of v. 13. Hope is connected with holiness in two ways:

(1) Hope issues in holiness (1 John iii. 3; 2 Cor. iii. 18).

(2) Holiness strengthens hope (Rom. xv. 33). So we regard these verses as giving us reasons for, or some of the companions of, hope.

1. **Our position of filial holiness.** "As children of obedience," *i.e.* those whose life of sonship has its source and characteristic in obedience (cf. Eph. ii. 2, 3; v. 6, 8; Rom. vi. 16). A strong reason for perfect hope.

2. **Our duty of definite holiness** (vv. 14, 15). Note the two sides of holiness:

(1) Negative: "Not fashioning yourselves according to the former lusts in your ignorance."

Not allowing your life to take its former sinful shape when you were ignorant of God and Christ. For "fashioning" cf. Rom. xii. 2 (Greek and R.V.) and 1 Cor. vii. 31 (A.V.). Also for "former" cf. Acts xvii. 30 and Eph. iv. 18, 22.

(2) Positive: "Be ye holy in all manner of conversation" (literally, "become ye holy"). "Conversation" means conduct, not speech. The old English word has become limited to talking; here it is "way of living," behavior.

3. **Our pattern of perfect holiness:** (v. 14) "Like as He . . . so be ye." God is here our Divine pattern. He requires conformity to Himself in those who are His (Eph. v. 1; 1 Thess. iv. 7; Heb. xii. 10). Verse 16 is quoted from Lev. xi. 44, 45, xix. 2, xx. 7.

SPECIAL STUDIES

1. **The calling of God:** "He which called you." Study the New Testament uses of "calling" (cf. Rom. viii. 30; 1 Pet. ii. 9, 21, iii. 9, v. 10; also Matt. xx. 16).

2. **The idea of holiness:** "Be ye holy," "I am holy." The root idea of holiness is separation, and refers to position, not condition. "Consecration" is the foundation thought. A holy person is "one who belongs to God" (John xvii. 17, "Sanctify"; Jude 3, "saints"). So the Temple as a "holy place" (Acts xxi. 28) was separated, devoted to God. Of course, the modern idea of purity follows out of the foregoing as a necessary consequence, but it is important to bear in mind the primary and fundamental

idea of *immunity* as contrasted with community, of *seclusion* as contrasted with inclusion. Every passage in the Old and New Testaments will bear out this interpretation.

Practical application:

1. Consider the height of holiness (v. 16). God's nature.

2. Consider the width of holiness (v. 15). "All manner of living" (nothing good excluded).

3. Consider the narrowness of holiness (v. 14). "Not fashioning yourselves," etc. (everything evil excluded).

35

HOLY FEAR
(1 Peter 1:17-21)

ANOTHER of the fruits of salvation now comes into view. As *hope* was the ketnote of vv. 13-16 so *fear* is the main idea of the present section. Note the contrast of the two thoughts and the balance and proportion of truth.

A. A PRACTICAL APPEAL (1:17)

"Pass the time of your sojourning here in fear."

1. **The meaning.** What is the fear here referred to? Distinguish between *dread* and *awe*. The former is slavish and non-Christian; the latter is filial and truly Christian. The former kind is referred to in 1 John iv. 18, and has no true place in Christian life and experience. The latter is an essential and necessary part of all true Christian living. "Godly fear" is reverential awe of God the Holy One and consequent suspicion of self and of all self's ways. Note the filial character of this fear ("Father," v. 17). Entirely compatible with our sonship and our freedom in grace (see Phil. ii. 12f., "with fear"; Heb. xii. 28, "reverence and godly fear"). Note also Paul's exhortations to "sober mindedness" and "soberness" (Tit. ii. 2, 4, 6; 1 Thess. v. 6; cf. Ps. cxxx. 4, lxxxix. 7, ii. 11).

2. **The scope.** "Pass the time" is cognate word with "conversation" (v. 15), and refers to the *whole life* in its outward action. "Walk up and down in fear." This element is to affect the whole life (cf. v. 1, R.V., "sojourners")." We are not settlers, only pilgrims.

3. **The power.** The attitude of godly fear is the needed balance to any possible abuse of the doctrines of free grace. It reminds us that "access," blessed and free as it is, is into the *holiest* (Heb. x. 19); that we come not only to a Father, but to God (Eph. ii. 18; Heb. xii. 23); and that "Holy and reverend is His Name" (Ps. cxi. 9). A needed lesson today. No slavish dread, but a reverential awe, as we rejoice in our privileges in Christ.

B. A PLAIN REASON (1:17)

"If ye call on Him as Father Who . . . judgeth." This is the first reason why the Apostle calls us to fear.

1. **God's relation to us:** "Father." The "if" implies "since as a fact," not any doubt of it. God's Fatherhood is thus a reason for filial fear. The Fatherhood here is of course the unique and special spiritual relation to believers (John i. 12; Gal. iii. 26).

2. **God's attitude to us:** "Judgeth." Note the striking collocation of "Father" and "judgeth." Not "loveth" or "pitieth," but *judgeth.* God's Fatherhood is a real one, not a sentimental, emotional, weak relationship. All true fatherhood has strong fibre

in it, and God's Fatherhood to believers is the pattern of all human relationships (see Heb. xii. 7-10). Note the absolute impartiality of this judgment: "Without respect of persons." No favorites, no bias. Study carefully the prominence of this thought all through Scripture from Deut. x. 17. Look up references and note especially 1 Sam. xvi. 7; Acts x. 34; Rom. ii. 11; Eph. vi. 9; Col. iii. 25.

3. **Our approach to God:** "If ye call" (cf. Rom. x. 13). Prayer is here assumed. The very fact that we have this access and approach is a reason for holy fear. Awe is a true characteristic of prayer.

But now the Apostle goes farther, and gives—

C. A POWERFUL INCENTIVE (1:18-19)

"Forasmuch."

Redemption is here urged as an incentive to fear. Such use of highest motives is frequent in the New Testament (Rom. xii. 1, "by the mercies of God"; Tit. ii. 10, 11, "adorning . . . for"; 1 Pet. i. 13, "Wherefore"). He appeals from highest privileges to lowest duties.

1. **A fact:** "Ye were redeemed." A fact without question, and therefore a *factor* and a *force* (cf. Luke xxiv. 21; Tit. ii. 14). Note particulars:

(*a*) Redemption implies slavery and bondage of sin.

(*b*) "From your vain manner of life" (cf. v. 15, action, not speech). "Vain" (cf. Rom. vi. 21; Eph. iv. 17 and v. 11). Empty of fruit or result.

(*c*) "Received from your fathers." This "empty" life had been handed down for generations: no real life apart from God in Christ. So today in unconverted and worldly families each generation inherits "emptiness" and aimlessness of life until converted.

2. An assured fact: "Ye know ye were redeemed." No doubt of it. Full assurance of faith (cf. Job. xix. 25; 2 Tim. i. 12; and St. John's First Epistle *passim,* especially 1 John v. 13). How can it be said "Ye know"?

(1) Christ died to redeem—A fact.

(2) The soul accepts Christ by faith—A fact.

(3) The Holy Spirit assures of acceptance—A fact. Result: "We know."

3. An important fact. "Not redeemed with corruptible things . . . but with the precious blood of Christ."

(*a*) "Not with corruptible things." Not even earth's costliest treasures can redeem (Ps. xlix. 7).

(*b*) "But with the precious blood" (cf. Exod. xii. 5; Isa. liii. 6, 7; John i. 29; Acts xx. 28; Rev. vii. 14). Precious to the Father Who gave. Precious to the Son Who died. Precious to the Spirit Who applies. Precious to the believer who receives. Precious to all eternity to God's praise and glory.

N.B.—Scripture clearly teaches ransom and redemption (Matt. xx. 28; 1 Tim. ii. 6), but is silent as *to whom* the price is paid. The price simply emphasizes the costliness.

Yet even this powerful incentive of the Apostle is driven home by further development of the thought of redemption in the form of—

178 / The Apostle Peter

D. A PRECIOUS ENCOURAGEMENT
(1:20-21)

1. **Redemption p u r p o s e d:** "Foreordained." Note the emphasis on this (cf. Acts ii. 23; Eph. i. 4; Rev. xiii. 8). Redemption is no afterthought.

2. **Redemption provided:** "Manifested" (cf. Heb. ix. 26; Heb. i. 3; 1 John iii. 5; I Tim. iii. 16).

3. **Redemption proved:** "God that raised . . . that your faith and hope might be in God" (cf. Rom. vi. 4; Heb. ii. 9 and xii. 2). The Resurrection is always spoken of as *God's* act, not Christ's (see Greek *passim*). It was God's justification and acceptance of the Lord and His sacrifice (Acts ii. 32f.).

4. **Redemption possessed:** "You who believe." Personal appropriation of redemption is necessary for complete fulfilment of God's purpose, and for our own salvation and holiness. This appropriation is "believe," and it is made possible "by Him."

SPECIAL NOTES

1. Study this and many other passages in full, as showing redemption as a motive to holiness. "The Cross of Christ condemns me to be a saint," said a native convert. Still better, "constrains" or "compels" us to holiness.

2. Note balance of truth here.

(a) Redeemed *from*.

(b) Redeemed *by*.

(c) Redeemed *for*.

36

BROTHER—LOVE
(1 Peter 1:22-25)

YET another fruit of salvation is now to be considered in addition to hope and fear. *Mutual love* among believers is the next subject of the Apostolic appeal.

A. THE EARNEST EXHORTATION (1:22)

"See that ye love one another . . . fervently."

1. **The nature of the call:** "Love one another," *i.e.* fellow-Christians. A subject very prominent in New Testament. Why? Doubtless due to the Master's words in John xiii. 34, 35: "a new commandment." Wherein was it *new?* Not in the *fact* of love, for love had been known and commanded in the Old Testament; nor really in the *standard* of love ("as I have loved you"), because the Old Testament standard of "love with all thy heart . . . soul . . . might" (Deut. vi. 5) was and is the highest possible standard for man. Note the emphasis on "one another" three times in two verses. The newness lay in the new *object* of love, fellow-believers. Up to that time such a tie was absolutely unknown. There had been love of kinship, of patriotism, of friendship, of pity and compassion; but this was a new

bond, and constituted a new ground of affection, *oneness in Christ,* which overleaps all barriers of blood, country, need, and affinity, and rests solely on relationship in Christ. Now note the prominence in the New Testament (John xv. 12, 17; Rom. xii. 10, xiii. 8; Eph. iv. 2, 3; Col. iii. 13, 14; Heb. xiii. 1, 16; Jas. ii. 15f.; 1 Pet. ii. 17, iii. 8; 2 Pet. i. 7; 1 John ii. 10, iii. 11-18). Especially note the word for this new love, "Philadelphia," in Heb. xiii. 1 and elsewhere. Up to the time of Christianity the word was only used of brothers *by blood*—so in the classics and Apocrypha (cf. *Ptolemy Philadelphus*). Now it is used for brothers *by grace.*

N.B.—Properly it is "brother-love," not "brotherly love." Not love *as though* brothers, but love *because* brothers (MASTERMAN *in loc.*). This love among Christians is intended to be a real power in home, congregational, and denominational life. "See how these Christians love one another!" was the astonished exclamation of the heathen in early days.

2. **The character of the call:** "Unfeigned." This love is to be real, genuine, no pretence about it (Rom. xii. 9; 2 Cor. vi. 6). No inward grudges while showing outward unity. Absolute reality of soul, speech, and service.

3. **The degree of the call:** "Fervently." The word means "intensely," stretched to farthest point (cf. iv. 8; Acts xii. 5, xxvi. 7; Luke xxii. 44, for the same word). See what great stress is laid upon this love.

4. **The source of the call:** "Out of a pure heart." R.V. omits "pure" ("from the heart").

This love must come thence if it is to be real and strong.

N.B.—Have we ever really allowed ourselves to take in this pressing duty? Do we thus love our fellow-Christians? Are they prominent in our lives? Do we find joy in their fellowship? (Ps. xvi. 3). Are we showing definite, practical love to them? If any say, Christians are often unattractive and angular, may they not feel this of us? And if our love may not be fully the love of complacency and true "alikeness," can we not love compassionately and express it in self-denying service, and so perhaps discover hidden excellences and even rub off their (and our!) angularities? What a power in the Church and world if only we had more of this "brother-love"! (Ps. cxxxiii. 1, 3).

B. THE DEFINITE OBLIGATION (1:22)

1. **A fact:** "Ye have purified your souls." "Souls" here stand for the whole moral and spiritual being (i. 9, iv. 19). For "purified" cf. Jas. iii. 17, iv. 8; 1 John iii. 3. Notice the purification is stated as a fact which is expressed, in the Greek, by the perfect tense, implying a fact of the past with abiding results in the present.

2. **A method:** "In your obedience to the truth." The "truth" is thus the secret and means of purity, and is often so stated in the New Testament (John xv. 3, xvii. 17, 19; Eph. v. 26). Contrast reference to "mind" (v. 13) and "ignorance" (v. 14), and see Eph. iv. 18. The fuller and more

constant the application of Divine truth to the soul, the greater will be the purity.

3. **A source:** "Through the Spirit." This is added in A.V., and suggests the Divine fount of truth and purity. Note the two titles, "Spirit of truth" (John xiv. 17) and "the Holy Spirit" (John xiv. 26) or "Spirit of holiness" (Rom. i. 4).

4. **A purpose:** "Unto unfeigned love of the brethren." "Brother-love" is thus the result of purity, just as hatred and enmity spring from sin and impurity (Tit. iii. 3; Jas. iv. 1).

We can thus understand from the earlier part of this verse the distinct obligation to brother-love ("seeing") which comes from the possession of heart purity through the truth of God.

C. THE GREAT CONFIRMATION (1:22-25)

The Apostle now associates with purity and love the general idea of the Christian life. He confirms the call to love by reminding them of the new life which is theirs, and shows that it must be exercised and expressed in love.

1. **The new life:** "Having been begotten again" (cf. v. 3; John i. 12, 13, iii. 5). Again the perfect tense is used, implying the fact of a life bestowed in the past which still abides. This life is thus at once a reason for brother-love and its opportunity (see the same argument in 1 John iv. 7, 8, v. 1).

2. **The simple means:** "Not of corruptible seed, but of incorruptible, through the Word." Just as in v. 22 purity comes through truth, so here life

springs from the Divine Word (cf. Luke viii. 11;
Jas. i. 18, 21; 1 John iii. 9).

3. **The Divine author:** "The Word of God,
which liveth and abideth." The Word is Divine,
and this alone is the secret of its power (John i.
13; Heb. iv. 12).

4. **The solemn reason:** Note the contrasts in
these verses between the corruptible and incorruptible, between the transient and permanent,
between the human and the Divine (cf. Isa. xl.
6-8). God's life is thus contrasted with human
life; and because the Divine life abides, our love
should be continuous. This is the point of the contrasts here introduced; a lasting life is a reason
for lasting love.

5. **The human channel.** "This is the Word . . .
preached unto you." It was through the Apostle
and others that this abiding Word of the Lord
had come to them and entered into their life (cf.
1 Cor. iv. 15). "Begotten you through the
Gospel."

37

SPIRITUAL PROGRESS
(1 Peter 2:1-3)

THE connection between chapters i. and ii. is obvious. Chapter i. deals with birth (vv. 3, 23); chapter ii. is concerned with growth (vv. 2, 5). Note carefully the "therefore" of v. 1, referring back to i. 23. Life must be followed by progress.

A. THE CALLS TO PROGRESS

1. **The need:** "That ye may grow." Growth is the natural, necessary, and gradual result of the Christian life. It is well illustrated by the required elements of bodily growth. In what respects do we expect the life of a child to grow? In strength, in attractiveness, in capacity, in experience. So also we require the counterparts of these four elements in spiritual growth.

2. **The means.** "Thereby," *i.e.* "spiritual milk which is without guile" (A.V.). "The sincere milk of the Word." Note again the reference to the truth as food (cf. i. 22, 23). Milk is a perfect food for children, containing all the elements necessary for building up the frame; so is the Word to the Christian. Food, in order to do its work, should be good

and suitable (cf. Isa. lv. 1). It should be simple, pleasant, and nutritious. Hence the two epithets, "sincere" and "guileless," the latter probably containing the idea of unadulterated or unwatered milk. This is a true description of God's Word in its strengthening, sustaining, and satisfying qualities. Its promises comfort. Its counsels guide. Its exhortations incite. Its warnings protect the newborn life.

3. **The end:** "Unto salvation" (see R.V.). The word is used as in i. 5-9, and refers to the completeness of salvation as realized hereafter. The Christian life is thus to be ever growing in vigor and power (Eph. iv. 13-16; 1 Cor. iii. 1-3, xiv. 20; Heb. v. 12-14, vi. 1; Phil. i. 10).

B. THE REASONS FOR PROGRESS

1. **Spiritual life:** "Babes" (cf. i. 23). The new life must have nourishment, and nourishment in agreement with its own nature. Hence the perfect accordance of the Divine life in the soul and the Divine life in the Word of God. When life is absent from the soul, Scripture is never enjoyed; but when life is present, Scripture is always desired.

2. **Spiritual immaturity:** "Newborn." this is a special reason for progress based on the dependence and helplessness of a recently born child. In 1 Cor. iii. 1-3 and Heb. v. 12-14 a distinction is drawn between the babe and the full-grown man. Here, however, the Apostle, writing probably years after their conversion, still speaks of

them as "newborn." In relation to eternity we are always "babes."

3. **Spiritual experience.** "Tasted." Note the force of "if so be" in this passage. It does not imply doubt, but means "since ye have tasted." The thought of tasting implies experience combined with pleasure (Ps. cxix. 97, 103, xxxiv. 8, xix. 10; Jer. xv. 16; Heb. vi. 4). "That the Lord is gracious." This, though quoted from Ps. xxxiv. 8, means more than simply good.

Dwell carefully on these reasons for growth in Christian life. Our life must be sustained; for sustenance there must be eating; for eating there must be appetite, and for appetite there must be a supply. This supply is found in the pure, unadulterated, abundant Word of God. Weakness among believers is often due, as bodily weakness is, to errors in diet. A "mixed" diet may be agreeable to the "old man," but it affords no real nourishment to the spiritual life.

C. THE CONDITIONS OF PROGRESS

The Apostle emphasizes the question of spiritual growth by calling attention to three prerequisites.

1. **Renunciation:** v. 1, "Putting away therefore," etc. The things mentioned here to be put away are five in number, and may refer to as many different forms of evil, though it is possible that the first is best rendered as in the R.V. by the general term "wickedness," and the others regarded as springing out of this. In any case all five seem specially to emphasize sins against

love as those which hinder growth. This is true of spiritual experience. The absence of brother-love is always associated with spiritual weakness as at once a cause and an effect. The putting away must be definite, deliberate, and permanent, as the Greek tense implies (cf. Eph. iv. 22, 25). The soul thus freed from hindrances will have opportunity to grow.

2. **Appropriation:** "Long for the spiritual milk." The word implies earnest desire, and of course presupposes a spiritual appetite. Bodily appetite affords a good illustration of spiritual desire in the three characteristics of: (1) Naturalness, (2) Heartiness, (3) Constancy; but in one respect the analogy fails, for spiritual appetite needs exhortation, and is not spontaneous, like bodily desire.

3. **Assimilation:** "Tasted." This spiritual taste of God's Word is only another way of speaking of meditation; and in all spiritual assimilation of God's Word there seem to be four true elements.

(1) Attention: the mind pondering and understanding the truth.

(2) Application: the conscience personally pressing home the truth.

(3) Aspiration: the heart desiring and praying in reference to the truth.

(4) Action: the will yielding to and obeying the truth.

38

SPIRITUAL PRIVILEGES
(1 Peter 2:4-6)

WE are still occupied with the fruits of salvation, but the Apostle now turns from the *duties* to the *privileges* of the Christian life. Verse 4 takes up the thought of v. 3, "Tasted that the Lord is gracious," and shows that the privileges now to be dwelt on are due to our union with Him. It is worth while to dwell on the power of *privileges* in relation to holiness and faithfulness. The privileges attract us, incite us, and impel us to progress. Now we consider growth as a privilege, and growth under the figure of a building instead of a life.

A. THE LORD'S GOODNESS (2:4)

1. **The person:** v. 4 "Whom." The essence of Christianity is our personal relation to the Divine person of our Lord.

2. **The life:** "Living stone" (Ps. cxviii. 22; Isa. viii. 14, xxviii. 16). We see here Peter's thought of his Master, and probably his own interpretation of his Master's words in Matt. xvi. 18 (cf. Eph. ii. 20). Note the combination of the two

ideas of life and stability in the phrase "living stone" (cf. Son of the *living* God," in Peter's confession, Matt. xvi.).

3. **The human rejection:** "Rejected indeed of men" (Acts iv. 11). Peter had very real cause to remember this fact.

4. **The Divine choice:** "With God, elect, precious" (Matt. iii. 17, xvi. 16, xii. 18; Isa. xlii. 1).

N.B.—Note carefully these elements of Peter's doctrine of the Person of Christ. They convey their own distinct impression and message.

B. THE BELIEVER'S EXPERIENCE (2:4-5)

1. **Personal approach to Christ:** v. 4, "Unto Whom coming." This means the whole movement of the inner life in the direction of Christ. Mind, heart, conscience, will, soul, all turned towards Him and approaching Him, and this continuously—"coming" (cf. Heb. iv. 16, vii. 25).

2. **Spiritual transformation through Christ:** v. 4, "Living stones." The same title is thus given to believers as to their Master, through Whose transforming grace they, in union with Him, become like Him, "living stones." They were formerly "dead in trespasses and sins," a mass of inert rock; now they are at once alive and strong.

3. **Divine influence of Christ.** v. 5, "Ye, being built up." This is the gradual progress of those who are united to Christ. A perpetual work of edification goes on. Collect and study the frequent references to growth under the figure of building (1 Cor. iii. 9; Eph. ii. 20-22; Jude 20).

C. THE PRACTICAL OUTCOME (2:5)

1. **Spiritual position:** v. 5, "House" (1 Cor. iii. 16; Heb. iii. 6). All believers together are regarded as the House of God.

2. **Spiritual purpose:** v. 5, "Priesthood." This also refers to the Church as a whole. Never in the New Testament is an individual believer spoken of in the singular number as a priest. Probably this suggests the need of exercising our priesthood in union with our fellow-believers in the Church as a whole.

3. **Spiritual privilege:** v. 5, "Sacrifices" (Rom. xii. 1; Phil. iv. 18; Heb. xiii. 15-16). New Testament sacrifices are always "spiritual," and include the sacrifice of ourselves, our gifts, and our praises.

4. **Spiritual possibility:** v. 5, "Acceptable to God, through Jesus Christ." Consider the glory of being able so to live and serve as to be acceptable to God. This shows what Divine grace can do.

N.B.—The fuller meaning of the believer's priesthood will come before us in v. 9. Meanwhile, note carefully the three thoughts which are applied to the Church. The Church is at once temple, priesthood, and sacrifice.

D. THE DIVINE WARRANT (2:6)

The Apostle goes on to confirm the foregoing teaching by referring to the Old Testament for proof and justification. The whole passage, indeed, is little more than a mosaic of Old Testament quotations, and clearly shows the Apostle's knowledge and practical use of the Scriptures of the Old Covenant.

1. **God's word and the Lord:** v. 6a, "Behold, I lay in Zion a chief cornerstone, elect, precious." God is the speaker, and this is His action in providing the Messiah, and His testimony to the Messiah as "elect, precious." The reference to "Zion" may suggest "grace" as contrasted with "Sinai," law. Our faith is thus founded on Divine acts, facts, and assurances.

2. **God's Word and the believer:** v. 6b, "He that believeth on Him shall not be put to shame" (Isa. xxviii. 16, viii. 14; cf. Rom. ix. 33; Eph. ii. 20). It is because our Lord is God's foundation that we are invited to believe on Him, and assured that we shall not be put to shame. Believing is a complex act and attitude of the soul whereby we (1) approach, (2) rest, (3) abide. And the more we respond to God's invitation the stronger will be our confidence in the great rock foundation of God's eternal love and grace.

39

SOME CONTRASTS
(1 Peter 2:7-10)

THE thought of Christian experience leads the
Apostle to describe a series of contrasts between
those who have come to Christ (v. 4) and those who
have not. Note five contrasts in the course of the
statement.

A. A CONTRAST OF ATTITUDE (2:7)

1. **Those who believe:** "For you therefore
which believe." Faith alone discerns, receives,
and enjoys spiritual realities.
2. **Those who disobey.** "Such as disbelieve."
Notice the contrast between belief and disbelief
or disobedience. Disbelief is more than unbelief,
and implies deliberate and wilful rejection of the
truth. Obedience is the submission of the whole
nature to Christ, and St. Paul speaks of the
"obedience of faith," that is, the obedience which
is the fruit of faith (Rom. i. 5, xvi. 26; Acts vi.
7; cf. 1 Pet. i. 2, 14, 22).

B. A CONTRAST OF EXPERIENCE (2:8)

1. **Honor:** "To you which believe is the preciousness." This word may be translated "pre-

ciousness" (cf. 1 Pet. i. 18, ii. 6). or it may be rendered "honor."

2. **Dishonor:** "A stone of stumbling." Quoted from Ps. cxviii. 22 (cf. Isa. viii. 14). Frequently referred to in New Testament (Matt. xxi. 42; Luke xx. 17; Acts iv. 11). The wilful disobedience brings about collision with God's foundation-stone, and the result is stumbling. St. Paul emphasizes the same solemn contrast in relation to Christ (2 Cor. ii. 16).

C. A CONTRAST OF POSITION (2:9)

This is the explanation of the preciousness or honor stated in v. 7.

1. **The believer's birth:** "Ye are an elect race" (Isa. xliii. 20; Gal. iv. 28). God's electing love and Divine gift of life are here emphasized.

2. **The believer's service:** "A royal priesthood" (Exod. xix. 6; Rev. i. 6, v. 10; cf. v. 5, "holy priesthood"). Does the term "royal priesthood" mean (1) priests who are kings or (2) priests who are at the court of kings? Perhaps both ideas are included, though the former seems more prominent. A priest is one who represents man to God (Heb. v. 1), and his twofold work is specially the offering of sacrifice and the duty of intercession. Notice the application to our Lord as our great High Priest in His unique sacrifice and Divine advocacy (Heb. vii. 25; 1 John ii. 2). From this we also see what priesthood means to Christians. Its privilege is nearness to God for

194 / The Apostle Peter

special service. The sacrifice of themselves and
of all that they have to God and His service, together with the ministry of intercession on behalf
of the world. Thus priesthood is not merely a
matter of privilege, but of responsibility and service. We must never rest content with insisting
upon our rights as priests in opposition to false
claims. We must see that we fulfil the duties also.

3. **The believer's nationality:** "An holy nation." The thought of the unique position of the
Jewish nation is here transferred to the Christian
Church, which, while drawn from all human na-
tionalities, nevertheless forms one holy or consecrated nation under the kingship of Christ (cf.
Eph. ii. 19, "fellow-citizens; Phil. iii. 20, "our
citizenship").

4. **The believer's relationship:** "A people for
God's own possession." The word implies pur-
chased or acquired possession (see Greek of 1
Thess. v. 9; Eph. i. 14; Heb. x. 39; and cf. Isa. xliii.
21). The "peculiar people" of the A.V. expresses
the old English idea of peculiar from *peculium,* private possession. The Church is God's *peculium.* The
word is allied to "pecuniary" (see Skeat's *Etymological Dictionary*). We are "bought with a
price," and so acquired for God's own possession.

D. A CONTRAST OF PRIVILEGE (2:10)

1. **The thought of the past.** The Apostle looks
back to his "darkness" (v. 9) out of which they
have been called. Darkness in Scripture is associated with sin, ignorance, gloom, sorrow, dan-

ger, shame, disease, death. All these are symbolical of the results of sin. In that dark past those to whom the Apostle is writing "were no people," they had no bond of union or unity, but were solitary units, enjoying no fellowship. The sinner, apart from Christ, knows nothing of *esprit de corps*. The result of all this was that in that dark and solitary past they had "not obtained mercy." This was the permanent state in which they had lived (cf. John iii. 36, "The wrath of God abideth on him").

2. **The thought of the present.** Instead of darkness it is "marvelous light" with those who are in Christ. Light in Scripture is associated with truth, joy, holiness, health, and life, and is indeed "amazing light." One result is that those who were formerly solitary are now united as the people of God under the headship of the Lord, and in fellowship with all other Christians (cf. Hos. i. 6, 9, ii. 23; Rom. ix. 25, 26). As the people of God they "have obtained mercy."

E. A CONTRAST OF PURPOSE (2:8-9)

1. **As to the disobedient:** v. 8, "Whereunto also they were appointed" (cf. Rom. ix. 33). Their stumbling was the consequence of their disobedience, and the result of this wilful rejection of God is His judicial abandonment of them to the uninterrupted results of their sin.

2. **As to the faithful:** v. 9, "That ye may show forth the excellences of Him Who hath called you." The word rendered "virtues" (A.V.) and "excellences" (R.V.) is only found in three other

passages in the New Testament (Phil. iv. 8; 2 Pet. i. 3, 5), in all of which it is rendered "virtue." Probably "excellences" is the best rendering here, suggesting a shining quality of light. In the LXX. the word is used to translate the Hebrew for "glory."

40

GENERAL COUNSELS
(1 Peter 2:11,12)

THE second great section of the Epistle (ii. 11—iv. 11) commences here with some general counsels, following the references to Christian privileges in vv. 3-10. It has been suggested that v. 11 seems to sum up i. 13—ii. 10, while v. 12 appears to look forward to ii. 11—iii. 12. The Apostle now makes an earnest and practical appeal to his readers.

A. THE NATURE OF THE APPEAL

1. **Its Negative aspect:** "Abstain." The call to purity of life. "Fleshly lusts" include all appetites, whether wrong in themselves or those that are only wrong through inordinate use (cf. Gal. v. 19-21). There is a striking contrast between these desires of the flesh and the desire of the newborn soul (v. 2).

Note also that in the young convert fleshly lusts may easily spring from genuine esteem and true affection, which may thus slide all unconsciously into evil.

2. **Its positive aspect:** "Your conversation" (cf. 1 Pet. i. 15, 17, 18, iii. 2, 16). The word, as elsewhere, is not to be limited to speech, but to the whole outward expression of character and conduct. "Honest" means "becoming," "suitable," and the Apostle thus appeals for becoming conduct in relation to non-Christians. "Among the Gentiles." The Christian life should be outwardly attractive to them "that are without" (Col. iv. 5).

B. THE TONE OF THE APPEAL

1. **The writer's affection:** "Beloved." Frequent in both Epistles.

2. **The writer's attitude:** "I beseech." Considering the Apostolic authority of St. Peter, we can see the true spirit of the man in this tender tone and spirit. It would give double force to his plea. This is a spirit which might well be imitated by all true teachers and pastors.

C. THE GROUND OF THE APPEAL

1. **He reminds them of their position:** "Sojourners" (cf. i. 17). They are in a foreign land, without civic rights, and therefore they must not conform to surrounding usages (v. 11), though at the same time their conduct is to be becoming (v. 12).

2. **He recalls to them their purpose:** "Pilgrims" (cf. i. 1). They are thus on the move, not stationary, and therefore cannot possibly stay to

entangle themselves with the life of the country through which they are hastening forward to their heavenly habitation.

D. THE REASONS OF THE APPEAL

1. **He dwells on the danger:** "Which war against the soul" (cf. Rom. vii. 23; Jas. iv. 1). This war against the soul implies hindrance and opposition to Christian progress as well as actual injury when fleshly lusts are yielded to.

2. **He emphasises the duty:** "Whereas they speak against you . . . they may by your good works . . . glorify God." A twofold duty is thus brought before them. (1) To disarm opposition. (2) To glorify God. "The day of visitation" is the Second Coming and seems to have special reference to judgment (cf. Isa. x. 3; Luke xix. 44). Some, however, think it may mean the day of salvation or opportunity in this life (Luke i. 68; Acts xv. 14; Matt. v. 16). In the phrase "which they behold" we have the suggestion of attentive watching and observation of Christians on the part of those who are outside. Hence the need of such exhortations as those about "walking circumspectly" (Eph. v. 15).

41

SUBMISSION TO THE STATE
(1 Peter 2:13-17)

AFTER the general counsels of vv. 11, 12, the Apostle proceeds to urge upon Christians the special duty of subjection or submission. Of the duty of submission he makes four applications to different aspects of Christian life.

(*a*) ii. 13-17. Submission to the State.
(*b*) ii. 18-25. Submission in the household.
(*c*) iii. 1-7. Submission in the family.
(*b*) iii. 8- 9 . Submission in general.

Our present subject is therefore concerned with the relation of the Christian to the State and Civil Government, and affords an interesting picture of early Christian life and duties. It is one of several passages in the New Testament on the relation of Christians to national life (cf. Rom. xiii. 1; Tit. iii. 1).

A. THE CLEAR COMMAND (2:13)

"Submit yourselves to every ordinance of man" (v. 13).

1. **The duty enjoined: "Submit."** This attitude is peculiarly and essentially Christian. It did not

enter practically into the life of the non-Christian world at that time or before the time of our Lord. Humility and submission were thought low and unworthy of human nature. Christ thus introduced a new thought and a new aspect of character into the world. The call to submission was also specially appropriate from the Apostle Peter when his own former unwillingness to be subject is remembered. This appeal therefore comes directly out of his own spiritual experience. How quickly and effectually this attitude of subjection one to another would solve the difficult problems of life!

2. **The expression of the duty:** "To every ordinance of man." Generally, this applies to every human institution or creation. Specifically, to the King (Emperor) or his accredited representatives. This attitude of the Christian to non-Christian and pagan institutions affords a striking instance of the true temper of the Gospel of Christ. How far are we to submit? Up to the point at which it becomes *sin* to obey. God must of course be kept first.

B. THE GREAT MOTIVE (2:13)

"For the Lord's sake" (v. 13).

Our relation to Him affects everything (Col. iii. 17). The precise force of this phrase, "because of the Lord," seems to include three aspects.

1. **To obey Him.** "The powers that be are ordained of God" and our submission to them is our acknowledgment of this in loyal obedience.

2. **To imitate Him.** When on earth He was subject, and the disciple is to be as his Lord (Matt. xvii. 27, xxii. 21).

3. **To glorify Him.** This spirit of submission cannot fail to bring glory to Him who "humbled Himself and became obedient."

C. THE DIVINE PURPOSE (2:15)

"For so is the will of God" (v. 15).

It is God's purpose that we should thus submit and be subject.

1. **The method of the purpose:** "By well-doing." This, beyond everything, is the reason why Christians are in the world, and nothing can possibly make up for the absence of "well-doing." It is at once the proof of our Christian profession and the best testimony to our Master.

2. **The result of the purpose:** "That . . . ye should put to silence the ignorance of foolish men." We saw (v. 12) the possibility of slanders against Christians. This is the only way to meet them effectually. "Ignorance" in this passage implies not merely the absence of knowledge, but a true lack of power to perceive, and thus the detractors, if unconvinced, may at least be silenced by the exhibition of Christian well-doing.

D. THE SPECIAL CHARACTERISTICS (2:16)

1. **The Christian as free:** "As free, and not using your liberty for a cloke of wickedness." No

truth is clearer in the New Testament than that of freedom in Christ (Gal. v. 1; John viii. 32, 36). Yet this liberty in Christ is always safeguarded and is "not a license to set at nought human law." Thus the Apostle guards against the possibility of a rebound from spiritual liberty to antinomian licence (2 Pet. ii. 18, 19; Jude 3, 4; Gal. v. 13).

2. **The Christian as faithful:** "But as the servants of God." The Christian is free, yet a slave, the bond-slave of Jesus Christ. There is no contradiction between these two aspects of life. "Whose service is perfect freedom" (*Cui servire est regnare*).

E. THE VARIED APPLICATION (2:17)

Some might question the possibility of subjection to such men as the heathen around them. The Apostle therefore goes into detail and shows a fourfold application of this principle of submission.

1. **Humanitarian:** "Honor all men." Give them that respect and deference which courtesy or custom demands. Estimate aright what is involved in true manhood and act accordingly. This honor of man as man is a noteworthy contribution to Christian ethics.

2. **Christian:** "Love the Brotherhood." This is the special application to their fellow-believers (i. 22, iii. 8, 4:8, v. 9). It is noteworthy that, whilst we are to *honor* all men, we are to *love* Christians.

3. **Divine:** "Fear God" (cf. i. 17). Reverential awe towards God will necessarily result in submission.

4. **National:** "Honor the King." An injunction all the more striking when we remember that (probably) Nero was on the throne. Loyalty to the institution is ever to be distinguished from confidence in the person who occupies the throne. Loyalty necessarily becomes harder if the monarch is personally unworthy, but though difficult, it is not to be regarded as impossible (Prov. xxiv. 21; Rom. xiii. 7).

42

SUBMISSION IN THE HOUSEHOLD
(1 Peter 2:18-25)

Now follows another application of the call to submission, this time in reference to domestic service and the relation of servants to their masters. It is another illustration of the "beautiful conduct" (Greek) urged in v. 12.

A. A PRACTICAL APPEAL (2:18)

1. **The persons addressed:** "Servants." These were slaves of the household.

2. **The duty urged:** "Be in subjection to your masters."

3. **The spirit shown:** "With all fear." The true characteristic of Christian submission is not the fear of punishment, but that spirit of deference and respect which shows itself in unquestioning obedience. This attitude is to be maintained even when masters are unreasonable and unsympathetic. "Not only to the good and yielding, but also to the crooked" (Greek). Note how Christianity hallows all life. The Bible is clearly against slavery, and yet the Apostle did not pro-

ceed to overturn a recognized social institution. He taught great principles which would gradually and effectually undermine it.

B. A DEFINITE REASON (2:19)

1. **He admits the possibility of injustice:** "Endure griefs, suffering wrongfully."

2. **He gives the explanation of the Christian attitude:** "For conscience toward God." This phrase may mean (*a*) a consciousness of God, *i.e.* the inspiration of His presence, or (*b*) a sense of duty towards God. The latter idea probably predominates, though both may be included.

3. **He shows the result which accrues:** "This is acceptable." The word rendered "acceptable" is "grace" and perhaps means "This is a mark of grace," a proof that God's grace is a power in their life (cf. Luke vi. 32, Greek).

C. FORCIBLE ARGUMENT (2:20)

1. He reminds them that **Suffering is sometimes deserved.** Even Christians manifest faults which involve them in trouble. There is no merit in patience under these circumstances.

2. He shows them that **Suffering is sometimes undeserved.** When, however, believers do well, and in suffering for it manifest patience, this receives God's gracious approval.

D. A POWERFUL MOTIVE (2:21)

Hitherto the Apostle has been dealing with the subject mainly on the plane of ordinary life and experience. Now he ascends to a higher plane and introduces motives which are intended to carry convincing force to every Christian heart.

1. **He declares the Divine call:** "For hereunto were ye called." Their existence as Christians involved the idea of suffering (Mark viii. 34; John xvi. 33; Acts xiv. 22; 1 Thess. iii. 4).

2. **He adduces the Divine model.** Our Lord's suffering is here used as an example which we are to follow. The thought combines the two ideas of the *headline* of a copy-book which we should imitate, and the *footprints* of a leader in which we should plant our own.

E. A PERFECT EXAMPLE (2:22-23)

Still more in detail does the Apostle adduce our Lord as the model Sufferer for His people to follow.

1. Negatively

(*a*) His suffering was unmerited. In deed, "He did no sin." In word, "Neither was guile found."

(*b*) His suffering was patient. In word, "He did not revile again." In word and deed, "He threatened not."

2. Positively

(*a*) His Divine act. "Committed Himself"; literally, "Kept handing Himself over." This was the secret of His endurance of suffering.

(*b*) The Supreme confidence. "Him that judgeth righteously." Amid all the suffering He knew that God was faithful.

In these two negative and positive aspects Christians are to follow their Master and find their peace amid affliction, in the continuous and continual surrender of themselves to Him Who ever abideth faithful (1 Cor. x. 13).

F. A DIVINE SAVIOR (2:24-25)

Notice how the Apostle's thought leads on step by step. He cannot rest content with bringing forward the example of our Lord, he must confirm it by a reference to His Divine work as the Saviour of man.

1. **The fact of the atoning death:** "Who His own self bare our sins in His own body on the tree" (cf. Isa. liii. 4, 11, 12; Heb. ix. 28). Each phrase of this sentence needs careful consideration. (1) The Person. "Who His own self"; (2) the humanity. "In His own body"; (3) the death. "Bare our sins on the tree" (cf. Col. i. 22, 23; Heb. x. 10; 1 Pet. iii. 18). In His Atonement our Lord was unique and has no followers.

2. **The purpose of the atoning death:** "That we . . . unto righteousness." Spiritual power is here shown to be the object of our Lord's death. The aspect of sanctification as the outcome of atonement is thus emphasized. The passage is parallel with Rom. vi., only that Paul deals with *sin* and Peter with *sins* (root and fruit). In 1 Pet. iii. 18 we have the thought of justification through atonement parallel with Rom. iii. It is important to notice and keep ever in mind the varied aspects of the purpose

of our Lord's death. The phrase in the Greek, "having died unto sins," is a striking expression implying absolute separation.

3. **The result of the atoning death** (vv. 24b, 25)

(*a*) Healing after disease. "By Whose stripes ye were healed."

Isa 53

(*b*) Home after wandering. "Ye were going astray like sheep, but are now returned." The description of our Lord as Shepherd and Overseer is a beautiful and appropriate ending to a passage which is so full of spiritual and practical teaching. As Shepherd He feeds, and as Bishop He keeps His people.

SUGGESTIONS

1. **High motives for humble duties.** It is very striking that such an ordinary and simple relation as that of master and slave should be emphasized in the light of the great sacrifice and example of Calvary. It is characteristic of the Apostle that he uses the highest possible motive powers in order to elicit the humblest of duties (cf. Tit. ii. 10, 11; 1 Cor. xv. 58, xvi. 1; Eph. iv. 25, v. 1; Phil. ii. 11, 12; Col. iii. 4, 5, 9, 10).

2. **The relation of the Lord's example to His Atonement.** It is only possible for our Lord's example to be reproduced in our life when we have accepted Him as our Atonement (v. 24a), our Life (v. 24b), and our Master (v. 25). The out-

ward Divine standard thus becomes realized by means of inward Divine strength.

3. **Ample power for all needs.** Dwell carefully on the fulness with which our Lord is here brought before us in relation to His death. He is at once our Peace, our Pattern, our Power, our Purity, and our Protection.

43

SUBMISSION IN THE FAMILY
(1 Peter 3:1-9)

THE Apostle is still occupied with various applications of the general idea of *subjection* or *submission;* vv. 1-7, in relation to wives and husbands; vv. 8, 9, in relation to all. These last two verses sum up the subject treated from ii. 13—iii. 7.

A. HOME LIFE (3:1-7)

1. **Wives** (vv. 1-6)

(*a*) The call.

(1) To submission: v. 1, "Be in subjection" (Eph. v. 22-24; Col. iii. 18; Tit. ii. 4, 5).

(2) To consistent life: v. 2, "Your chaste behaviour coupled with fear" (cf. ii. 8). Religious observances were greatly mixed up with heathen home life. Hence the difficulty in the case of a Christian wife and a non-Christian husband, and the need of special care (cf. 1 Cor. vii. 10-16).

(3) To becoming appearance (v. 3). Not to be understood as an absolute prohibition of the things mentioned, but the need of relative proportion between the outward appearance and the inward life.

The Christian woman is to avoid excessive "smartness," "slovenliness," and "dowdiness," and is to cultivate neatness and appropriateness of apparel.

(4) To genuine character: v. 4, "The incorruptible apparel of a meek and quiet spirit" for the "hidden man" (cf. Rom. ii. 28, 29, vii. 22; 2 Cor. iv. 16).

(*b*) The motives.

(1) Influence on husbands: v. 1, "They may without the word be gained," that is, without talking about spiritual things, and certainly without spiritual lecturing or "nagging," the husband may be attracted by the behaviour of the wife.

(2) Approval of God: v. 4, "In the sight of God of great price." Character is always so (cf. 1 Tim. ii. 8-12).

(3) Examples of former days (vv. 5, 6). "Holy women (v. 5), "Sara" (v. 6). "Holy" here, as elsewhere, means "belonging to God," "consecrated."

(*c*) The outcome: v. 6, "Whose children ye now are," that is, they became so when they accepted Christianity. The concluding words, "not put in fear by any terror," refer to the fear caused by persecution. They are to obey God rather than man when the alternative has to be faced. Contrast the fear of v. 2.

2. Husbands (v. 7)

(*a*) The call.

(1) To considerateness. "Dwell with your wives according to knowledge," that is, with a real spiritual perception of duty and relationship.

(2) To honor. "Giving honor." Note the force of this in view of the subjection (v. 1; cf. ii. 17).

(*b*) The motives.

(1) Natural. "The weaker vessel." The phrase may apply to the wife as the weaker person or may have the special application of 1 Thess. iv. 4.

(2) Spiritual. "Joint heirs of the grace of life" (cf. Eph. v. 25; Col. iii. 19). Note the beautiful completeness of these two motives. He is to care for her because she is weak, and he is to honor her because she is a Christian.

(*c*) The outcome. "That your prayers be not hindered." Married life and fellowship are intended as a help, not a hindrance, to spiritual progress.

B. GENERAL LIFE (3:8-9)

Now comes the closing summary of these counsels to submission, and there is a twofold application.

1. **In relation to Christians** (v. 8). Notice the five characteristics. (1) Like-minded; (2) Sympathetic; (3) Brother-loving; (4) Tender-hearted; (5) Kindly, or humble-minded. All these elements are marked by the general spirit and attitude of submissiveness.

2. **In relation to non-Christians** (v. 9). Notice two characteristics." (1) Negative: in action, "not rendering evil for evil"; in word, "or reviling for reviling." (2) Positive: but "contrariwise blessing." These again show the spirit of submissiveness, and hereunto are Christians called that (when they have so done) they should inherit a blessing.

44

TRUE LIFE
(1 Peter 3:10-17)

THE Christian life in relation to the world around
has been briefly delineated in verse 9. The subject
is now amplified in various particulars from the Old
Testament, and from their own experience and
needs. Consider the following points in illustration
of *a true Christian life.*

A. AN ASPIRATION
(3:10, cf. Psalm 34:12-16)

1. **The life described:** "Love life and see good
days." This clearly indicates the duty of enjoying the Christian life and not feeling weary of it.
It is no necessary reference to material prosperi-
ty, but rather to spiritual satisfaction (cf. Deut.
xxxiii. 23).

2. **The way indicated:** "He that will," *literally,*
wills, determines. This shows that such a life is
possible in spite of all untoward circumstances.
True spiritual satisfaction is independent of our
surroundings (cf. our Lord's phrase about loving life, John xii. 25).

B. AN EXPLANATION (3:10-11)

Three particulars are given as to the conditions required for realizing this true life.

1. **Our speech.** Two kinds of evil are to cease; that which is *bad* and that which is *unnecessary.*

2. **Our action:** "Turn away from evil and do good." The twofold attitude; negative and positive.

3. **Our purpose:** "Seek peace and pursue it." Every energy is to be bent in this direction.

C. AN INCENTIVE (3:12)

1. **Towards God:** "The eyes of the Lord . . . and His ears . . . supplications." God always keeps His promises.

2. **Against evil:** "But the face of the Lord . . . evil." God always fulfils His threatenings.

D. AN INQUIRY (3:13)

The point of this question is that they are not to forget God's overruling power even though they are persecuted. No real harm can possibly accrue to the follower of Christ.

1. **The necessary condition:** "Zealous of that which is good."

2. **The implied consequence:** "Who is he that will harm you?"

E. AN ASSURANCE (3:14a)

A further encouragement in the case of persecution.

1. **He states a contingency:** "But, and if ye should" (cf. Matt. v. 10).

2. **He describes a result.** "Happy are ye" (cf. Acts v. 41).

F. AN APPEAL (3:14a-16)

Now comes a full and detailed explanation of their true attitude to the heathen around. He makes an urgent and yet affectionate sevenfold appeal.

1. **For courage:** v. 14, "Fear not . . . troubled, . . ." (cf. Isa. viii. 12, 13).

2. **For reverence:** v. 15, "Sanctify in your hearts Christ as Lord." Note the root idea of "sanctify," meaning to "separate or consecrate." "Put Christ first as Lord of your life."

3. **For readiness:** v. 15, "Being ready always." Note specially this call to constant preparedness.

4. **For confession:** v. 15, "To give an answer." No hiding of the light, but frank testimony when required.

5. **For conviction:** v. 15, "The reason concerning the Hope." Their outward confession is thus to be based upon inward conviction. They are to have a reason, not an excuse. Mark once more the Apostle's emphasis on hope. His outlook was ever on the future, and Christianity was to him prominently a hope.

6. **For humility:** v. 15, "With meekness and fear." This shows the true attitude; strong conviction and bold confession, but with an entire absence of boastfulness and vainglory.

7. **For sincerity:** v. 16, "Having a good conscience." Their life was thus to keep pace with their speech, and their conscience within was to bear testimony to the reality of their convictions and the frankness of their confession. This "good conscience" would express itself in "good manner of life" (cf. iii. 21, i. 15).

G. AN ENCOURAGEMENT (3:17)

Beautifully does the Apostle now close this description of a true life by describing:

1. **Its secret:** "If the will of God should so will." God's will covers and includes everything, either as active or permissive. To the Christian there are no second causes. "The devil may bring, but God sends."

2. **Its satisfaction:** "It is better that ye suffer for well doing than for evil doing." Well doing is God's will, and whatever be the consequences accruing from this, God's will is always best.

45

SUFFERING FOR RIGHTEOUSNESS
(1)

(1 Peter 3:18-22)

THE immediate subject is suffering for well doing, and the connection between v. 18 ("because") and v. 17 is close and definite. The Christians are called to bear their sufferings as Christ bore His, and then, like His, their sufferings will issue in blessing and lead to eternal glory. This is the general line of thought of the whole passage, apart from the details of interpretation which have occasioned so much difficulty. Before considering the passage, more minutely it will be well to keep in mind the two points which are vital to any true understanding of the section.

1. The main thought of the preceding and following contexts.

(a) vv. 14-17. Suffering for righteousness. This is illustrated by the example of Christ (v. 18) and its happy issues (v. 19-22). Note carefully that there is no break in the reasoning from v. 14 to v. 22.

(*b*) iv. 1-5) The succeeding context is an appeal to holy endurance in suffering, which is also pointed by the example of our Lord.

2. The apparently abrupt and unnecessary introduction of Noah and the people of his days must be explained and accounted for in the light of the general thought of the entire passage.

A. THE SUFFERINGS OF CHRIST: THEIR CHARACTER (3:18a)

1. **The fact:** "Christ also suffered . . . being put to death in the flesh."

There is thus an exact correspondence between the sufferings of Christ and Christians in relation to bodily pain and anguish, leading often in the case of Christians even to death.

2. **The nature:** "For sins, the righteous for the unrighteous." The character of the sufferer in suffering without real cause is also paralleled by Christians suffering simply for their faith. Yet here the phrases also include certain aspects of our Lord's atoning sufferings "for us . . . for the unrighteous") in which Christians necessarily have no share.

3. **The purpose:** "That he might bring us to God" (cf. Eph. ii. 18, iii. 12). This clear purpose of the Atonement as issuing in union and communion with God may also find its parallel on a much lower level, in the fact that the sufferings of Christians may convict and lead to God those who cause them to suffer.

B. THE SUFFERINGS OF CHRIST:
THEIR CONSEQUENCES (3:18b-21)

1. **Death was followed by resurrection:** "Being put to death in the flesh, but quickened in the spirit." There is a clear antithesis between "flesh" and "spirit" (cf. 1 Tim. iii. 16., R.V.). The reference is not, as in A.V., to the Holy Spirit. This evident antithesis makes it clear that the quickening must refer to the resurrection. "Made alive as to spirit." His human spirit was never dead and so could not be "made alive" or "quickened." The term is equally inapplicable to the Holy Spirit, and we are therefore left with the sole interpretation of the spiritual quickening of His resurrection. The passage is thus exactly parallel to Rom. i. 3, 4. By the resurrection our Lord received a "spiritual body" and with it a wonderful access of spiritual quickening power. Already Son of God before the resurrection, He was thereby designated "Son of God *with power,*" that is, with the gift of power to exercise and to bestow upon others (cf. "spiritual body" in 1 Cor. xv. 44).

2. **Resurrection was followed by activity:** "In which [spirit] also to the spirits in prison He went and preached." The preaching, therefore, whatever it was, occurred *after the resurrection,* for evidently the preaching was subsequent to the quickening. Four different views are however taken of this preaching.

(*a*) That it was by our Lord *through Noah* (*i.e.* the Lord's Spirit preached through the patriarch)

to the antediluvians who were disobedient while the
Ark was being prepared. This is the view suggested
by the A.V. by the use of the proper noun "Spirit"
and the difference made in the prepositions *"in* the
flesh" and *"by* the Spirit." Most of the older com-
mentators favor this interpretation. It seems difficult,
however, to see why the Apostle should suddenly go
back two thousand years in a context which certainly seems to suggest a preaching *subsequent to* the
suffering. It also makes it difficult, if not impossible,
to see how our Lord could thus have been an example to the Christians, and this is the main point
of the passage.

(*b*) That it was a proclamation by our Lord *in
Person* to the people who had been disobedient in
the time of Noah. This proclamation may have been
an offer of salvation or a mere announcement of the
completion of His redemptive work. If it was an
offer of salvation, two questions at once arise. (1)
Why was the offer made to these only and to no one
else? (2) How is it that such an offer, after this life
is over, is absolutely opposed to the general sense of
Holy Scripture?

(*c*) That it was a proclamation by our Lord *in
Person* to the fallen angels (spirits in prison), an-
nouncing even to them the victory of our Lord over
sin (cf. 2 Pet. ii. 4, 9; Jude 6). It is urged that the
term "spirits" is never used in Scripture of human
beings, without qualification or clear statement in
the context (Heb. i. 7, xii. 23). It is difficult to fit in
this view with the general thought of the context of
suffering leading to blessing and glory.

(*d*) That it was a proclamation by our Lord, *through His Apostle,* to those who were in the prison house of sin (see Isa. xlii. 5-7, xlix. 8, 9, lxi. 1). Of this sinful race, the people of the time of Noah were examples. This view has the great advantage of accounting for the reference to Noah. The result of his preaching for one hundred and twenty years was only eight souls saved, while the preaching of our Lord in the spiritual quickening following His resurrection had resulted in the marvelous success of three thousand souls in one day. There is thus on this view a "suppressed apodosis" which makes "the passage intelligible and points the contrast." The difference of result between Noah's preaching and the apostolic preaching of Christ is thus explained by the accession of spiritual power which accrued to our Lord by the resurrection when He was "quickened as to spirit." From this comes the next point of the comparison.

3. **Activity followed by blessing.** Our Lord's sufferings were thus followed by renewed activity and an influx of power and blessing to thousands of souls. So, implies the Apostle, would it be with those to whom he was writing. Their sufferings for Christ, so far from really injuring them, would be overruled for blessing and glory.

The reference to the time of Noah suggests to the Apostle a further analogy between the Flood and Christian baptism. "Which also, after a true likeness, doth now save you, even baptism, not the putting away of the filth of the flesh, but the interrogation of a good conscience towards God through the resurrection of Jesus Christ." The true point of the analogy lies, not in the water, but in the antitype or spiritual counterpart of the water. Noah was not saved by the water, but having escaped the water he was saved in the Ark. Perhaps the best rendering of the words is "which [water], in the antitype, doth now save you," that is, the spiritual counterpart of the water is the means of our salvation, water being an outward sign of a spiritual cleansing. This is evident from the careful qualification which follows, "not the putting away," etc. Thus, the water in baptism is not the antitype of the Flood, but the spiritual antitype of baptism saves us (cf. R.V. margin). For "antitype" see Greek of Heb. ix. 24. The phrase in A.V., "answer of a good conscience," R.V., "interrogation," is thought to be either (1) a request to God for a good conscience, or (2) an inquiry addressed to God by a good conscience. Though there is not much etymological warrant for it, the best word seems to be "decision," thus expressing the *surrender* of the soul to God as it accepts God's salvation "through the resurrection of Jesus Christ."

C. THE SUFFERINGS OF CHRIST: THEIR CULMINATION (3:22)

1. **His exalted position:** "Who is on the right hand of God, having gone into heaven."
2. **His supreme dominion:** "Angels . . . subject unto Him." These two points carry the thought to its climax. As our Lord suffered, and these suf-

ferings resulted in this Divine glory, so will it be with Christians who suffer for conscience" sake. They also shall come at length to God's everlasting glory.

SPECIAL NOTES

1. The view of this passage taken above is necessarily stated with great brevity, and with avoidance of detail in order to prevent the general thought of the whole section from being lost in a long discussion of particulars. It does not pretend to solve every difficulty, though it is urged that its weaknesses are not fatal, and its advantages by strict adherence to the context are certainly much greater that those of other explanations. All other suggestions seem to introduce extraneous topics which are unwarranted by the context and by the general tenor of the New Testament. The one point above all others to be borne in mind is that "quickened as to spirit" refers to the resurrection, and this necessarily involves a preaching subsequent to that event. If it be thought that "spirits in prison" cannot fairly refer to the human race in the prison house of sin, it may be pointed out that the LXX of Isa. xlii. 7, where the reference is undoubtedly to sin, has the exact Greek word *phulakee* of this passage. For fuller discussions of this view see *Expository Discourses on First Peter,* by John Brown, D.D., and a valuable article by Dr. R. Gordon Balfour (*Expository Times.,* VII. 356), which summarizes and re-states the view with great force, and to which the above exposition is much indebted.

Even though the precise clue has now been lost, it is significant that the Apostle refers to the matter in an ordinary way as something quite familiar to him and his readers.

2. It is necessary to be on our guard against drawing inferences from this passage which are foreign to the context and purpose.

(1) As to the *preaching.* If this were taken to mean probation after death it is difficult to understand its uniqueness in the New Testament, and still more difficult to understand why this second offer should be limited to those antediluvian sinners. It is manifestly unfair and impossible to argue by inference from these to others.

(2) As to *baptism.* It is only by an absolute limitation to the words "baptism doth also now save" that an erroneous view of that sacred ordinance can be obtained. The context clearly states the true view in its balance of the human and Divine sides of salvation.

3. The personal application to Christians is the most important thought. They are to be like their Master. (*a*) In suffering, (*b*) in consequent blessing, (*c*) in subsequent glory. As His sufferings, so far from putting an end to His influence, really enhanced His power, so shall it be with His followers. "The blood of the martyrs is the seed of the Church," and those who suffer on behalf of Christ shall find their sufferings fruitful in blessing to others and glory to God.

46

SUFFERING FOR RIGHTEOUSNESS (2)

(1 Peter 4:1-6)

THE main subject of iii. 14-17 is now resumed, and again the call comes to suffer for righteousness' sake. This involves certain clear consequences in Christian living, and has a direct and definite bearing on holiness and separation from sin.

A. THE DIVINE EXAMPLE (4:1)

1. **The fact:** "Christ hath suffered."

2. **The form:** "In the flesh."

B. THE URGENT CALL (4:1)

1. **To spiritual action:** "Arm yourselves" (cf. Eph. vi. 11; Rom. vi. 11).

2. **To spiritual equipment:** "With the same mind" (cf. Heb. iv. 12 for this word, which means "thought"). What is this "thought"? Some think "the very thought which sustained Him in His suffering," namely, that He was suffering accord-

ing to the will of God (iii. 17), or it may mean that the very fact of His suffering is the Christian's armour. Perhaps, however, the word "for" in v. 1 should be rendered "that," and thus be introductory to the particular thought here referred to. "Arm yourselves also with the same thought that he . . . ceased from sin."

C. THE PRACTICAL POWER (4:1-2)

1. **The negative side:** "Ceased from sin that ye no longer should live . . . to the lusts of men." The idea is that when we accept and appropriate to ourselves our Lord's sufferings we become so identified with Him that the career of sin is broken and brought to an end. We are so identified with Christ's victory that it becomes ours and we have died to sin in His death (cf. Rom. vi. 1-11; 2 Cor. v. 14). Note here again the association of Christ's sufferings with sanctification. It is Peter's equivalent of Paul's teaching in Rom. vi.

2. **The positive side:** "But [live] to the will of God." Christians are to arm themselves with this thought of perfect victory over sin in order that they may live to God (Rom. vi. 10-13, 22).

D. THE DEFINITE REMINDER (4:3)

1. **Their past life depicted.** Note the two classes of sins, impurity and intemperance, which are regarded as arising out of idolatry.

2. **Their past life changed:** "May suffice." No longer are they living to the will of the Gentiles, but to the will of God.

E. THE PRESENT EXPERIENCE (4:4)

1. **Misconception:** "They think it strange that ye run not with them." Former associates cannot understand the transformations of grace and the new tastes of the Christian.

2. **Calumny:** "Speaking evil of you." This is the result of misconception and the unwillingness of the Christians to associate with them in sin.

F. THE GREAT ENCOURAGEMENT (4:5)

In the midst of all this misunderstanding and these false charges on the part of their non-Christian acquaintances the following words are intended to cheer and strengthen them.

1. **The future tribunal:** "Who shall give account." On that day the Christian attitude will be justified when their opponents stand before God.

2. **The Divine attitude:** "Him that is ready to judge." This is intended to show them that God is not forgetful of them. He not only "judges righteously" (ii. 23), but He is ready to do so, for the judgment time is imminent and the Christian's salvation is ready to be revealed (i. 5).

G. THE SPECIAL ILLUSTRATION (4:6)

As a further explanation and encouragement to endure patiently for Christ's sake the Apostle now introduces a reference to others who had suffered like them.

1. **The preaching:** "The Gospel was preached even to the dead." That is, dead when the Epistle was written, not dead when the Gospel was preached to them. They had fallen under human tribunals because of their confession of Christ, and mention is here made of them to show that they were not failures, but that God's purposes concerning them were nevertheless accomplished.

2. **The purpose:** "That they might be," etc. Perhaps the best rendering of these words is "in order that although condemned according to the will of men as to flesh, they might nevertheless live according to the will of God as to spirit"; that is to say, they are not lost and destroyed, but are still living unto God.

N.B.—Some interpreters suggest that the reference is to the spiritually dead, who are thus used as a motive to holiness. It is interesting to notice the parallels here with iii. 18:—

Flesh.	Christ put to death in the flesh.	Christ quickened in spirit.
Spirit.	Christians judged in the flesh.	Christians live in spirit.

SUGGESTIONS

1. **The warfare of the Christian life.** Evidently real and constant.

2. **The armour of the Christian life.** Adequate.

3. **The distinctiveness of the Christian life.** Note the definite contrast between "living to the lusts of men" and "to the will of God." The difference between "the time past" and "the rest of your time" is unmistakable, and shows what Christianity must always mean in its distinctive attitude against sin.

4. **The inspirations of the Christian life.** Two thoughts are again emphasized to cheer and hearten: the example of their Master and the glory that is to follow.

47

AN URGENT CALL
(1 Peter 4:7-11)

At this point it is necessary to review ii. 11—iv. 7. Its keynote, as we have seen, is submission. The present verses form a summary of the whole passage with special reference to Christian character and duty. Even here the underlying thought of submission is present, as shown in love and service. At the same time, the passage seems to be somewhat transitional, looking forward to the next section as well as backward on the preceding context.

A. THE STIRRING APPEAL (4:7-11)

1. To personal holiness (v. 7)

(*a*) Sober-mindedness. "Be ye therefore of sound mind." The word implies self-control, and is very prominent in the Pastoral Epistles of St. Paul (cf. 2 Tim. i. 7).

(*b*) Watchfulness. "Be sober unto prayer" (cf. i. 13). A call to vigilance and alertness of spirit with a view to greater earnestness and power in prayer.

2. **To brotherly love** (vv. 8, 9). Again this element of true Christianity is made prominent by the Apostle (cf. i. 22, ii. 1-17).

(*a*) Its supremacy (v. 8). "Before all things."

(*b*) Its fervency (v. 8). "Being fervent" (cf. i. 22).

(*c*) Its sincerity (v. 8). "Love covereth a multitude of sins" (cf. Prov. x. 12; Jas. v. 20). As quoted by James the phrase seems to mean "Love covers by atoning," but Peter's use suggests "Love is blind to faults."

(*d*) Its reality (v. 9). "Using hospitality." Note the prominence of hospitality in the New Testament (Rom. xii. 13; 1 Tim. iii. 2; Tit. i. 8; Heb. xiii. 2). Christian intercourse between the Churches called for this exercise as well as the social ostracism involved in the confession of Christ. Note the proof of this reality in the phrase "without murmuring." Yet even in apostolic days there were those who abused hospitality by "sponging" on strangers (2 Pet. ii. 3; Jude 12).

3. **To definite service** (vv. 10, 11). Observe how this Christian work follows naturally from our inward character of holiness and our outward attitude of brother-love.

(*a*) The foundation of service. "Received the gift," that is, a faculty or power of grace from God for the purpose of service. The word rendered "gift" is only here found outside St. Paul (cf. 1 Cor. xii. 8-10).

(*b*) The scope of service. "Each one hath received" (cf. Rom. xii. 3, 6; Eph. iv. 7). It shows that not a single Christian was exempt from this privilege and consequent duty.

(*c*) The standard of service. "According as each one hath received." God only expects gifts proportionate to blessings, but He does expect nothing short of this.

(*d*) The obligation of service. "As good stewards" (cf. Luke xii. 42; 1 Cor. iv. 1; Eph. iii. 2; Tit. i. 7).

(*e*) The variety of service. "Manifold grace of God." As grace comes in varied ways so also are its manifestations in service.

(*f*) The quality of service. "As it were oracles; as of the strength." Thus in *speech* and *action* our service is to be the very best we can render. "With thy might." And yet it is not "thy might" but the strength which God supplies (Jas. i. 5; 2 Cor. ix. 8-11).

N.B.—"Speaking as it were oracles" may mean "with the authority, gravity, sincerity that characterises them," or else "as the oracles of God require us to speak." Both ideas, however, can be included.

B. THE SOLEMN MOTIVE (4:7)

1. **The great expectation:** "The end of all things" (cf. i. 5, 6, iv. 5; Rom. xiii. 11, 12).

2. **The personal experience:** "Is at hand" (cf. Jas. v. 7-9). Their circumstances suggested that the coming was imminent, and therefore the time for such holiness, love, and service was short.

234 / The Apostle Peter

N.B.—Can this refer to the approaching end of the Jewish economy as viewed by the Apostle a few years before A.D. 70?

C. THE SUPREME PURPOSE (4:11)

1. **Life's glorious meaning:** "That God in all things may be glorified through Jesus Christ" (cf. 1 Cor. x. 31; Phil. i. 11 and ii. 11).

(*a*) The fact. "Glorified." Glory is the manifestation of splendor. God's splendor is to be manifested in our lives.

(*b*) The extent. "In all things." Nothing is too trivial or outside the scope of God's glory.

(*c*) The possibility. "Through Jesus Christ." It is in union with Him that it becomes possible thus to glorify God.

2. **Life's practical expression:** "Whose is the glory and dominion for ever and ever." This is the Christian's doxology.

(*a*) He gives God the glory.

(*b*) He ascribes to God the power.

(*c*) He testifies to the perpetuity of the grace and glory of God in Christ. Thus by lip and life, in the present and in the future, the Christian life is to be a doxology to God.

48

STEADFASTNESS
(1 Peter 4:12-19)

A NEW section commences here with the same tender appeal as in ii. 11, "Beloved." It extends to v. 11, and consists of renewed exhortations to constancy and fidelity in several aspects and applications. The present passage has almost entire reference to patient endurance and steadfastness in the midst of persecution. Keeping this thought in view, the following aspects of the teaching are to be noted.

A. AN EXPERIENCE (4:12)

"The fiery trial among you, which cometh upon you."

1. **A present trial.** Note R.V. here, which clearly suggests ((following the Greek) that the trial was already upon them, and not, as in A.V., still future.

2. **A severe trial.** The original word rendered "fiery trial" is used for "furnace" in Rev. xviii. 9, 18, A.V. "burning." Perhaps "trial by fire" would be a better rendering (cf. Luke xii. 49; 1 Pet. i. 6, 7). This, then, was the present and terrible experience of those to whom the Apostle wrote, and the trial was evidently general: "among you."

What was the cause of it? This leads the Apostle to give.

B. AN EXPLANATION (4:14,16)

1. **Reproach** (v. 14). They bore the Name of Christ, and the trial was due simply to the fact of their association with their Master (cf. Matt. v. 11; Heb. xi. 26).

2. **They suffered as Christians** (v. 16). This is only another way of stating the same fact. For the term "Christian" cf. Acts xi. 26, xxvi. 28. It is only found three times in New Testament. It is generally thought to have been given as a nickname by their enemies, though the original word "called" in Acts xi. 26 (a rare word in New Testament) is elsewhere uniformly expressive of a Divine oracle or utterance. May not this term have really been given by God to mark the followers of Jesus, and to distinguish them from all others? Certainly by the time of this Epistle the name is more than a nickname, while very soon after the close of the first century it was the universal appellation used by Christians themselves. Consider carefully what it means today, both at home and abroad, to suffer simply because we are Christians. Circumstances vary, but the fact is the same in all ages.

This leads the Apostle to give

C. AN ENCOURAGEMENT (4:12-16)

1. **Against perplexity** (v. 12). They were not to think it "strange" that this trial was upon them as though it was a chance, and as though they were forgotten of God. One reason for it

was "to prove" them (cf. i. 6, 7; Heb. xii. 6). The strangeness would also be removed with the thought that their Master had also suffered, and that they were only following Him.

2. **Against disheartenment** (v. 13). They were partakers of Christ's sufferings, and were therefore not to be discouraged (cf. i. 11, ii. 21, iii. 18, iv. 1; 2 Cor. i. 7; Phil, iii. 10; Col. i. 24). In so far as they were thus in fellowship with their Master, they were not to be discouraged, but to "rejoice."

3. **Against shame** (vv. 14-16). Doubtless they were tempted to be afraid and ashamed of their religion in face of all this fiery trial. To meet this possibility the Apostle calls them "blessed" (v. 14) (cf. iii. 14), and tells them that "the Spirit of glory and of God was already resting upon them" (Isa. xi. 2) like the Shechinah glory on the Tabernacle. They were therefore not to be ashamed, but to glorify God in this Name of their Master (v. 16, R.V.).

N.B.—Note this title of the Holy Spirit, only found here; cf. "God of glory" (Acts vii. 2), and "Lord of glory" (1 Cor. ii. 8).

But this threefold encouragement was not all that he had to put before them, for he now brings forward.

D. AN EXPECTATION (4:13,17)

1. **Of glory** (v. 13) (cf. i. 5, 7, 13). They are to look above and beyond the suffering to the glory that is to follow (ch. v. 1).

2. **Of joy.** In that glory they will experience not merely the joy of the present (v. 13a), but

exultation (see Greek). Their joy will then express itself in the most active and energetic forms.

3. **Of judgment.** This was also part of their expectation and intended to balance and safeguard their joy in anticipation of glory. The Apostle evidently regards the judgment as imminent (v. 17), and considers that it would be a sifting-time for the people of God. This "judgment" has no reference to sin, which was settled on their acceptance of Christ (John iii. 18, v. 24, R.V.; Rom. viii. 1). It refers to the testing of their faithfulness since conversion and their use of God's grace (1 Cor. iii. 13-15). Christians will not appear before the Great White Throne (Rev. xx. 11), but before the judgment seat of Christ" (Rom. xiv. 12; 1 Cor. iv. 2-5; 2 Cor. v. 10). This thought of judgment was intended as an incentive to faithfulness, especially in view of trial and persecution.

E. AN EXAMINATION (4:15,17,18)

With a view to the thorough testing of the Christian life of those addressed, the Apostle proceeds to apply certain tests to their practical, every-day living.

1. **As to the present** (v. 15). There was possibly danger of their confusing suffering for righteousness' sake with suffering brought on by their own sin or folly or blunders. Hence the injunction that they were not to suffer "as a murderer, or a thief, or an evildoer, or as a meddler in other men's matters." The expression is

emphatic. "Let no single one of you." The reference to "meddling" is expressed in a word only found here in the New Testament and not in earlier Greek literature. Probably it was coined by St. Peter. Literally it means "other people's overseer," and so applies to intrusion into the sphere of work allotted to another. This may refer to the excessive and unwise zeal of many of those early Christians, who thus brought trouble and suffering unnecessarily upon themselves. The word is rendered "busybody" in the A. V. (cf. 1 Thess. iv. 11; 2 Thess. iii. 11; 1 Tim. v. 13). We must beware of the danger of thinking we are suffering for Christ when our troubles are due to our own faults.

2. **As to the future** (vv. 17, 18). The two solemn questions here asked and purposely left unanswered convey their own searching message to the consciences of Christians. They clearly imply the solemnity and responsibility of being Christians (cf. Ezek. ix. 6, "Begin at My sanctuary"; Amos iii. 2). The phrase "scarcely saved" may be illustrated from the LXX. of Prov. xi. 31. It shows the possibility and power of temptation and evil that salvation can be spoken of in these terms. God is perfectly holy and just, and none should be readier to realize and acknowledge this than those who are His.

F. AN EXHORTATION (4:19)

The Apostle now sums up the whole question of suffering for righteousness' sake, by indicating the true attitude of the believer. In this verse we have what has been rightly called the germ of the whole Epistle.

1. **The condition required:** "Suffer according to the will of God." This is one prerequisite in the matter before us, and it is only with reference to such that the exhortation applies. Note the blessed secret suggested by "according to the will of God." When this is realized as the explanation of otherwise perplexing circumstances, the soul is at rest and peace.

2. **The act enjoined:** "Commit their souls." A better rendering would be "deposit" (cf. Ps. xxxi. 5; Luke xxiii. 46; 1 Tim. i. 18; 2 Tim. i. 12, 18). See a similar word in ii. 23, "Hand over." The tense of the word is the present and implies "keep continually depositing."

3. **The proof afforded:** "In well doing." This is "the outward and visible sign" of the deposit of the soul with God, and this explains the present tense of the injunction. It is by continual and continuous well doing that we show the reality of our soul-committal to God.

4. **The guarantee assured:** "Unto a faithful Creator." The title of Creator implies power, while the epithet "faithful" reveals to us that character of God which assures us that that which we have committed to Him He is both *able* and *certain* to keep. "God is faithful" is the foundation of Christianity which is thus based on the impregnable rock of the character of God (1 John i. 8-10; 1 Thess. v. 24; 2 Thess. iii. 3; 1 Cor. x. 13; Heb. x. 23, xi. 11; 2 Tim. ii. 13; Rev. xix. 11).

49

SHEPHERDS AND FLOCK
(1 Peter 5:1-7)

THE Apostle now resumes his general counsels on the reciprocal duties of Christians (see iv. 7-11) after the special topic of suffering for righteousness' sake (iv. 12-19). First comes an appeal to the shepherds, and then to the flock.

A. A CALL TO FAITHFULNESS (5:1-4)

The reference to "elders" is evidently to the pastoral ministry existing in the churches. The term seems to have been derived from the Jewish synagogue (Luke vii. 3). It is first used of Christian ministry in Acts xi. 30, though we have no trace of the actual origin and first appointment. The term was interchangeable with that of "bishop" or "overseer" (Acts xx. 17, 28; 1 Tim. iii. 1-7; Phil. i. 1). The various aspects of the Apostle's call are worthy of the closest possible study.

1. **It is based on personal appeal** (v. 1)
(*a*)   Notice its tender tone, "I beseech." Instead of using apostolic authority he encourages and exhorts.

242 / The Apostle Peter

(*b*) Its sympathetic attitude. A threefold description of himself. "Fellow-elder," that is, in age and in service for Christ. "Witness of the sufferings of Christ," constituting a special ground of appeal (cf. Acts i. 8, 21, 22). "Partaker of the glory that shall be revealed," a fact almost always associated in this Epistle with the sufferings which were in such marked contrast (i. 5, 13, iii. 18, 22, iv. 13).

2. It is concerned with genuine motives (vv. 2, 3)

(*a*) He reminds them of the nature of their work. "Tend the flock of God." A reminiscence of John xxi. 16 (cf. ii. 25). Mark the emphasis upon the need of food and the duty of feeding. Christian life must be strong and vigorous.

(*b*) He reminds them of the spirit of their work. Three ministerial dangers are mentioned. (1) Officialism; that is, constraint and compulsion in service instead of spontaneity and desire of will. Doing duty simply because it must be done. (2) Avarice; serving simply for gain instead of disinterestedness and genuine eagerness of spirit (cf. 1 Tim. iii. 8: Tit. i 7; Heb. xiii. 5). (3) Pride; temptation to ambition and domineering instead of a conciliatory spirit (cf. Matt. xx. 25). In opposition to these the Apostle emphasizes *willingness, eagerness,* and *personal example.* The phrase in R.V., "making yourselves examples," is, literally, *becoming* examples. The minister should be ever growing, always "becoming" more experienced, and so constantly affording a fuller exemplification of the true life. Of these three ministerial temptations Calvin (quoted by Lillie) says *tria vitia quae plurimum obesse solent.*

N.B.—Note the twofold description of the Church, "the flock of God" (v. 2); "the charge allotted" (v. 3) (cf. Acts xx. 28; Deut. x. 9).

3. **It is inspired by glorious prospects** (v. 4)

(*a*) The Lord's coming (cf. ii. 25). Note the threefold description of our Lord as Shepherd in the New Testament. The Good Shepherd Who dies (John x. 11); the Great Shepherd Who is raised from the dead (Heb. xiii. 20); the Chief Shepherd Who will come again (v. 4).

(*b*) The servant's reward. "The unfading crown of glory" (cf. i. 4; 1 Cor. ix. 25; 2 Tim. iv. 8; Jas. i. 12).

B. A CALL TO LOWLINESS (5:5-6)

1. **A special appeal:** "Ye younger be subject unto the elder" (cf. ii. 18; iii. 1). The "younger" evidently refers to age and possibly the "elder" also, whether in the ministry or in the congregation (cf. 1 Tim. v. 1, 2, 17).

2. **A general exhortation**

(*a*) Humility to one another (v. 5). "Be clothed"; the word, only found here, is a picturesque expression, referring to the white garment or apron worn by slaves (cf. John xiii. 4, 5). The reason given for this humility is because of the attitude, respectively, to the proud and humble (cf. Prov. iii. 34, LXX.; Jas. iv. 6). Note the beautiful paradox of the Christian life of everybody being subject to everybody else (cf. Rom. xii. 10; Gal. vi. 2; Eph. v. 21; Phil. ii. 3).

(*b*) Humility towards God (v. 6). The Christian's true position is "under the mighty hand of God," the place of power and blessing (Deut. iii. 24; Job. xxx. 21; Ps. cxviii. 15, 16). Such a position necessarily calls us to humble ourselves. God's purpose in all this is "that He may exalt you (Luke xiv. 11) in due time." Not when we desire or expect, but when He wills (cf. i. 7, iv. 13).

C. A CALL TO TRUSTFULNESS (5:7)

As the human side has been thus emphasized in regard to faithfulness and lowliness, the Apostle now balances these aspects by dwelling on the Divine encouragement given to such a true Christian life, more particularly in view of their sufferings and difficulties at the hands of non-Christians.

1. **The deep need:** "All your anxiety" (R.V.) (cf. Matt. vi. 25, 27, 31, 34). The word implies distraction of mind and heart in view of conflicting emotions.

2. **The definite counsel:** "Casting all your anxiety upon Him" (cf. Ps. lv. 22). A definite act of unreserved surrender and appeal to God (cf. iv. 19).

3. **The Divine encouragement:** "Because He careth for you." The very heart of the Gospel is here. "God with us." "He saw them toiling in rowing" (Mark vi. 48; Exod. iii. 7, 8).

SUGGESTIONS

1. The light shed on Christianity

(*a*) Its prominent graces. Humility, sincerity, confidence. Note especially the emphasis on passive graces as contrasted with the active virtues of pre-Christian days. Particularly dwell upon the pagan thought of humility as betokened by the Latin, *humilis,* and the Greek, *tapeinos* both suggesting that it is grovelling and humiliating. Christianity transforms the idea and glorifies it, showing that humility is never equivalent to humiliation.

(*b*) Its absolute reality. Dwell upon the searching tests applied to the ministry, and note how Christianity concerns itself first and foremost with motives. "Motives make the man."

(*c*) Its spiritual powers. Dwell on the fulness of the teaching about God's relation to His people. He careth, He giveth, He exalteth, He cometh, He rewardeth.

2. The light shed on the Apostle's character

Few passages more clearly show the wonderful transformations of grace affected in Simon Peter, especially in regard to (*a*) Tenderness; (*b*) Humility; (*c*) Sympathy.

50

CLOSING COUNSELS
(1 Peter 5:8-14)

THE Apostle draws to a close with a few final words of counsel and cheer. Like the entire Epistle, this section is concerned with the difficult and trying position of the Christians and their need of personal watchfulness and Divine grace.

A. CONCLUDING EXHORTATIONS (5:8-9)

1. **The earnest call:** "Be sober, be watchful." This twofold call reminds them of the need of sobriety and self-control in the use of this world (i. 13, iv. 7) and of vigilance in view of opposing dangers. The contrast between this counsel and that of verse 7 is suggestive. Our trust in God's care does not set aside the duty of watchfulness.

2. **The solemn reason:** "Your adversary the devil." The word "adversary" is literally an opponent in a court of law (Matt. v. 25; **Luke xii.** 58, xviii. 33). The meaning of "Satan" is accuser (cf. Ps. cix. 6; Zech. iii. 1; Rev. xii. 10; cf. "devil," that is, slanderer). The Apostle is clear as to the fact of an adversary and as to the nature and persistence of his power. The figure of a roaring

lion suggests cruelty and strength (Ps. xxii. 13). Contrast the idea of a serpent suggesting deceit and craftiness.

3. **The urgent duty**: "Whom withstand steadfast in your faith." The call to resist is always and uniformly the attitude of the Christian (Jas. iv. 7; Eph. vi. 11, 12). When resisted the devil always flees. The teaching of Scripture is clear that the devil cannot possibly overpower the believer apart from his personal will. "Steadfast in your faith" refers to our "established confidence in Christ" (cf. Acts xvi. 5; Col. ii. 5). Faith in Christ leads to steadfastness, and this gives power to resist.

4. **The helpful reminder**: "Knowing that the same sufferings are accomplished in your brethren." These suffering and persecuted Christians were thus taught that they were not alone in the world, but that they were members of one great family and fellowship in whom there was community of experience. The word "accomplished" (literally, brought to an end, perfected) contains the further encouragement that the sufferings were not to last for ever.

B. FINAL ENCOURAGEMENTS (5:10-11)

1. **The character of God**: "The God of all grace." A unique title in the New Testament, revealing God as the source of all needed power and strength for daily living. "The God of every grace" suggests the variety of the Divine supply to meet the variety of human requirements.

2. **The purpose of God:** "Who called you unto
His eternal glory in Christ." Another allusion to
the glory so prominent in this Epistle. The "calling" is a characteristic word in the New Testament (cf. our Lord's phrase "Many are called,"
Matt. xxii. 14). St. Paul's use of calling included
the believer's response to that call (1 Cor. i. 9;
Rom. viii. 28, 30). It is always associated with
God's eternal purpose. This calling finds its due
sphere "in Christ"; the phrase in this verse seeming to refer to the calling and the glory.

3. **The will of God:** "After that ye have suffered a little while." Yet another allusion to their
sufferings, with the cheering thought that it was
only for "a little while." God's people are only
to be tested "according to the will of God." No
outside power can go beyond or contrary to that.

4. **The power of God:** "Shall Himself perfect,
stablish, strengthen you." This is to be read as a
promise (R.V.), not as a prayer (A.V.). Note the
three (or A.V. four) elements of the promised
power. (1) Perfect, *i.e.* adjust. (2) Stablish, *i.e.* confirm. (3) Strengthen, *i.e.* endue with power. (4)
Settle, *i.e.* fix on a foundation. A beautiful and complete picture of the true Christian life. It is first ad-
justed in its right relation, it is then established in
its true position, it is then endued with needed power
for active service, and the outcome is a solidity of life
and character.

C. CLOSING SALUTATIONS (5:12-14)

1. **The messenger:** "By Silvanus." Doubtless
the Silas of Acts xv. 22, 40, and the Silvanus of

2 Cor. i. 19; 1 Thess. i. 1; 2 Thess. i. 1. One of the close connections between the two great Apostles, Peter and Paul. Note Peter's description of Silas and his testimony to him, "our faithful brother as I account him."

2. **The purpose:** "I have written unto you briefly, exhorting and testifying that this is the true grace of God; stand ye fast therein." This is the purpose of the Epistle, in a few words calling attention to (1) the true grace of God; (2) his own personal encouragement and assurance thereto; (3) his exhortations to stand fast therein (cf. Gal. v. 1; Eph. vi. 13). These three threads, as we have seen, run through the whole Epistle: God's grace; Peter's testimony; the believer's duty.

3. **The greetings:** "She that is in Babylon . . . Mark my son." Probably a church is referred to, not an individual in "she that is in Babylon" (cf. 1 Cor. xvi. 19; 2 John 1. 13). Probably Babylon is to be taken literally, and the greeting is from the church there to the churches in Asia Minor (i. 1). Mark is another close connection between Peter and Paul (cf. Acts xii. 25, xiii. 5, xv. 37; Col. iv. 10, and note the influence of Peter in our second Gospel). "The kiss of love" was the usual greeting among the early Christians (Rom. xvi. 16; 1 Cor. xvi. 20).

4. **The benediction:** "Peace be unto you all that are in Christ." The echo of his Master's words "In Me ye might have peace" (John xvi. 33).

51

INTRODUCTION TO THE SECOND EPISTLE

BEFORE proceeding to the detailed study of the Epistle, it is useful to consider it as a whole. It should be read through at one sitting, so as to gain a general idea of its substance; then it might be read again, with special reference to the following points.

A. THE WRITER

1. **Notice his claim for himself** (i. 1). He at once speaks of his personal relation to Christ and the spiritual experience arising out of that relationship.

2. **He is an old man** (i. 13, 14). Evidently the end of life is at hand. He speaks of his death as imminent.

3. **He remembers early days.** The reference to his approaching death (i. 14) is clearly a reminiscence of the conversation between our Lord and himself recorded in John xxi. 18. He also refers in vivid detail to the Transfiguration (i 16-18). It is noteworthy that his companion on that occasion, John, also remembers and records his ex-

perience of the Transfiguration (John i. 14; cf. Luke ix. 32; "They saw His glory").

4. **He alludes to his First Epistle** (iii. 1)

5. **He refers to St. Paul** (iii. 15, 16). A striking testimony to the importance of St. Paul's writings in the Church at that early date. Also a beautiful and significant indication of the relations of the two great Apostles.

B. THE READERS

1. **They are generally referred to as Christians** (i. 1, 4)

2. **They are not recent converts** (i. 12)

3. **They evidently know the Old Testament** (i. 20, ii. 4-8, 15). Whether they are Jewish or Gentile Christians it is impossible to say.

4. **They were in danger from false teachers** (iii. 2, 17). The special peril was antinomianism: men who professed godliness and were in works reprobate (cf. Tit. i. 16; 2 Tim. iii. 5, 8).

C. THE PURPOSE

A careful study of the Epistle will elicit the following points as included in the Apostle's object in writing.

1. **To remind them of pressing needs** (i. 12, iii. 1, 2, 8, 17). Notice the special emphasis on "remembrance."

2. **To exhort them to holy diligence** (i. 5, 10, iii. 14). Another keynote to the Epistle is found in the word "diligence."

3. **To warn them against deadly error** (ii. 1, iii. 3, 17). The danger felt was from those who in words pretended to be Christian teachers, but whose deeds disgraced their profession.

4. **To encourage them to spiritual progress** (i. 8, 11, iii. 14, 18). The stress laid on "knowledge" and growth is another prominent feature of the Epistle.

This alternation of reminder and warning with exhortation and encouragement runs through the Epistle and shows the double purpose and aim. We see it summed up in iii. 17, 18 in the negative and positive aspects.

D. ANALYSIS

Like the First Epistle, there is no clear and logical outline of the thought, but the general idea seems to be expressed in three main sections, each introduced by a personal reference to the writer himself, and each containing a special exhortation based on a special reason.

1. i. 1-11. Divine gifts (1-4) and human response (5-11). Exhortation to earnestness (i. 5, 10).

2. i. 12-ii. 22. Divine prophecy (16-21) and human travesty (ii. 1-22). Exhortation to watchfulness (i. 19, ii. 20).

3. iii. 1-18. Divine words (2) and human mockery (3-10). Exhortation to holiness (iii. 11, 14, 17).

E. GENERAL NOTES

1. The relation of 2 Peter to the First Epistle

(*a*) The keynote of 1 Peter is HOPE in view of present sufferings.

The keynote of 2 Peter is KNOWLEDGE in view of present dangers (i. 2, 3, 5, 8, 12, 20, ii. 20, 21, iii. 3, 5, 8, 18).

(*b*) 2 Peter is thus a sequel (iii. 1) written by reason of different circumstances in the life of the churches.

(*c*) Several points of contact between the two Epistles should be noted.

(1) The end in view. (1 Pet. i. 5, iv. 7; 2 Pet. iii. 10, 12).

(2) Prophecy and its definite source (1 Pet. i. 10, 11; 2 Pet. i. 20).

(3) The fewness of those saved from the flood (1 Pet. iii. 20; 2 Pet. ii. 5, iii. 6).

(4) A use of "virtue" unique in the New Testament (1 Pet. ii. 9; 2 Pet. i. 3).

(*d*) Several points of contrast are also evident.

(1) In 1 Peter Christ's death, and resurrection are emphasized; in 2 Peter Christ's present exaltation.

(2) 1 Peter is full of Old Testament quotations and allusions; 2 Peter has no quotations, only allusions to historic facts.

2. The relation of 2 Peter and Jude

(*a*) There is an evident use of one writing by the author of the other (cf. 2 Pet. ii. 1-16 and Jude 4-11).

(*b*) Authorities differ as to which is earlier; some arguing for the priority of Jude (Alford, Salmon), others for the priority of 2 Peter (Lumby, Bigg).

3. **The language and style**

Very picturesque and poetical, with quite a number of unusual words. Both Epistles are alike in these respects. Other differences between them in regard to language and style are doubtless due to differences of topics and, it may be, of amanuenses.

F. SPECIAL NOTE

Those who desire to study the questions connected with the genuineness of this Epistle are referred to Alford, Lumby (*Speakers' Commentary*); Caffin (*Pulpit Commentary*); and especially to Bigg's recent and very able discussion (*International Critical Commentary*). There do not seem to be any other alternatives than genuineness and forgery. Either it is the work of the Apostle, or else his name is used to give it a show of authority. The latter alternative is surely no real instance of "an obvious literary device" (*Hastings' Bible Dictionary*), but rather would be a case of "religious fraud." The writer's claims to the name and position of Apostle and to personal knowledge and experience of the Transfiguration are too definite and solemn to admit of question. The Church of God has hardly been deceived all through the ages.

52

DIVINE PROVISION
(2 Peter 1:1-4)

THE opening words (vv. 1, 2) are marked by characteristic thoughts which run through the entire Epistle, *e.g.* "faith," "righteousness," "Saviour," "knowledge." Then a foundation is at once laid (vv. 3, 4) in a statement of the Divine gifts by which alone the Christian life becomes possible.

A. PERSONAL SALUTATIONS (1:1-2)

1. The writer of the Epistle

(*a*) His name. "Simon Peter"; the double name recalls the twofold aspect of his life before and after discipleship to Christ. This combination of names is not found in St. Mark or the Acts. The recurrence to the old name of early days is an illustration of an old man's reminiscences. The Greek is "Symeon," as in Acts xv. 14.

(*b*) His title. "Servant and Apostle" (cf. Rom. i. 1; Tit. i. 1). Here we see the two sides of the Christian life—his general relation as a servant, and his special position as an Apostle. The order of the two is worth noting.

2. The recipients of the Epistle

(*a*) Their spiritual position. "To those who have obtained like precious faith with us." In 1 Peter the Christians are first of all described by their geographical position. Here they are only described by their spiritual experience. "Precious" is a word characteristic of Peter's two Epistles (cf. 1 Pet. i. 7, 19, ii. 6). Wherein is faith "precious"? Because it links us to God; it keeps us safe in God, and is the channel of spiritual purification (Gal. ii. 20; Heb. xi. 6; 1 Pet. i. 5; Acts xv. 9). In speaking of "like precious faith with us" the Apostle shows his tact and courtesy in putting himself on the same level of spiritual privilege. "Obtained" implies by Divine lot or bestowment. The word is used in Luke i. 9; John xix. 24; Acts i. 17, A.V.

(*b*) Their spiritual foundation. "Through the righteousness" is literally "in the righteousness" and probably refers to God's righteousness as the object of our faith (cf. Rom. i. 17, iii. 26). Some think, however, that the reference here is not to the righteousness which makes atonement, but to the justice of God which gives equally to all.

Note the use of the phrase "God and Saviour"; probably both referring to our Lord, as there is no article with the second substantive (cf. i. 11, ii. 20, iii. 2, 18; Tit. ii. 13).

3. The greeting of the Epistle

(*a*) The substance of the prayer. "Grace and peace."

(*b*) The measure of the request. "Be multiplied."

(*c*) The source of the supply. "In the knowledge of God and of Jesus our Lord; cf. similar greetings in 1 Pet. i. 2; Jude 2; and note the spiritual order of grace and peace as cause and effect. The reference to "knowledge" as the source of grace and peace at once brings into prominence the keyword of the Epistle. The Greek is *epignosis,* full or mature knowledge. It is found fifteen times in St. Paul; once in Hebrews; four times in 2 Peter, and nowhere else. All spiritual grace comes from our personal knowledge and experience of God (cf. v. 3). They that know their God shall be strong" (Dan. xi. 32). "Acquaint now thyself with Him and be at peace" (Job xxii. 21). "Life eternal to know Thee" (John xvii. 3).

B. DIVINE PROVISION (1:3-4)

1. **Its character:** v. 3, "Life and godliness." Note these two elements of Christian experience. The possession of *life* and its expression in *reverence.* The latter word is found here and in iii. 11, and is specially characteristic of the Pastoral Epistles. The order of these two is also to be noted.

2. **Its spirit:** vv. 3, 4, "Granted unto us." Notice the emphasis in this representation of the thought of God's free and full gift. Not human merit, but Divine love characterizes this provision.

3. **Its extent:** v. 3, "All things." Everything for the commencement, continuance, and completion of the Christian life is thus provided. The

certainty and encouragement of this assurance is evident.

4. **Its guarantee:** v. 3, "His Divine power." This is the adequate and permanent assurance to the believer of the provision for his life.

5. **Its secret:** v. 3, "Through the knowledge of Him that hath called us by His own glory and virtue." This Divine provision only becomes available in union and communion with God. Note again the reference to "knowledge" and let it be remembered that "knowledge" always implies much more than intellectual perception, for it includes spiritual experience. Note R.V. of last clause, "By His own glory and virtue." The Greek word rendered "virtue" (1 Pet. ii. 9; Phil. iv. 8) is used by the LXX. to translate "glory." Here it evidently refers to the Divine nature, and perhaps is best rendered "energy." The thought is that God calls us by His own character of *glory* and *power*. The A.V. is clearly inaccurate here.

6. **Its channel:** v. 4, "His precious and exceeding great promises." These are God's means of bringing us into the knowledge of Him and thereby of providing all things for life and godliness. The promises of the Gospel include all, whether of the old or new Covenants (cf. 2 Cor. i. 20, vii. 1; Gal. iii. 14, 22; Eph. i. 13; Heb. ix. 15, x. 36, xi. 9, 11, 13, 39).

7. **Its purpose:** v. 4, "That through these ye might become partakers of the Divine nature." The promises thus introduce us to fellowship

with God, whereby we are made partakers of His
Divine life. For "partakers" cf. 2 Cor. xiii. 14;
Phil. ii. 1; Heb. xii. 10. This is the culmination of
redemption: union and communion with God (1
John i. 3).

8. **Its prerequisite:** v. 4, "Having escaped the
corruption that is in the world by lust." Here the
Apostle indicates their former experience, and at
the same time their full deliverance from it. Like
Lot, they have escaped (ii. 18, 20). It is only after
having escaped that God's purpose of fellowship
becomes possible.

TOPICS FOR STUDY

1. **The revelation of God to man**
(*a*) His righteousness (v. 1).
(*b*) His knowledge (v. 2).
(*c*) His power (v. 3).
2. **The gifts of God to men**
(*a*) Faith (v. 1).
(*b*) Grace (vv. 2, 3).
(*c*) Promises (v. 4).
3. **The purposes of God for man**
(*a*) Life (v. 3).
(*b*) Godliness (v. 3).
(*c*) Union (v. 4).

53

A CALL TO DILIGENCE
(2 Peter 1:5-11)

THE Apostle has laid the foundation in the Divine gifts (vv. 1-4) provided in sufficiency and bounty for life and godliness. Now comes the complementary truth of the need of human response to Divine provision. The keynote of the passage is "diligence" (vv. 5, 11).

A. THE EARNEST CALL TO DILIGENCE (1:5)

1. **The Divine foundation:** "Yea, and for this very cause." This phrase refers back to the Divine gifts already mentioned. These constitute the foundation of diligence and the adequate incentive to earnest effort.

2. **The human condition:** "In your faith." This is the one prerequisite of all progress in the Christian life. There must be faith at the root of all else. Note the emphasis laid on "faith" as the basis of Christianity all through the New Testament.

3. **The special responsibility:** "Adding on your part." The word in the original, of which the R.V.

thus gives the meaning, points to a very real personal relation and response to the Divine gift. God multiplies (v. 2) grace and peace, then the believer adds diligence (v. 5). Note also the phrase "all diligence." The words mean "haste," *i.e.* eagerness based on earnestness.

B. THE CLEAR MARKS OF DILIGENCE (1:5-7)

1. **Their elements.** Seven elements of diligence are mentioned, showing the completeness of God's gift (v. 3). "Virtue," *i.e.* manly energy or courage (cf. v. 3; 1 Pet. ii. 9; Phil. iv. 8). These are the only instances of the word in the New Testament. In the LXX. it is used to express Hebrew "Glory and Praise." Hence the A.V. of 1 Pet. ii. 9—"Knowledge." Another emphasis on this great requirement (cf. vv. 2, 3)—"Temperance," *lit.* self-control.—"Patience," *lit.* endurance. Note the relation of these two words. Power over that which is within (self-control); power over that which is without (endurance). "Godliness" or "reverence," a prominent word here and in Pastoral Epistles. "Love of the brethren"; another link with the First Epistle (1 Pet. i. 22, ii. 17, iii. 8, iv. 8, v. 9). The special love of Christians one to another. "Love"; the general attitude of all men.

2. *Their order.* Note that faith is the foundation and love the culmination, and every grace in between springs out of faith and is intended to be expressed ultimately in love. For faith as foundation

cf. Rom. xiv. 23. For love as crown cf. 1 Tim. i. 5. Each element is the foundation or soil of the other.

3. **Their completeness.** They cover all our relationships and attitudes. The first two are active graces, the second two are passive, the next refers to God, the sixth to the Church and the last to all men. As there is this necessary connection between each one, we should note that each and all are expected to be in every Christian: not some in some Christians, and others in others (see Gal. v. 22). "Fruit of the Spirit" not fruits. The nine elements constitute one cluster to be exemplified in every Christian life. So is it here with these seven marks of diligence.

C. THE BLESSED RESULTS OF DILIGENCE (1:8)

1. **Permanence of character:** "If these things are yours." The word implies "yours permanently." It is stronger than the ordinary verb "to be" and indicates an abiding possession. The importance of character as the result of persistent action cannot be too overrated.

2. **Depth of character:** "And abound." This addition shows the extent to which the Apostle would lead his readers. The terms indicating "abundance" and "fulness" are very frequent in St. Paul with reference to the depth and extent of Christian experience and life (cf. Rom. xv. 13, 14).

3. **Reality of character:** "They make you to be not idle nor unfruitful unto the knowledge of our

Lord Jesus Christ." Reality of character is seen in this description; "not idle nor unfruitful," and the purpose of this is indicated in the words "unto the knowledge of our Lord Jesus Christ." Whatever permanence, depth, and reality become ours as the result of diligence, the outcome will be an increasing experience of our Master and an ever-deepening fellowship with Him.

D. THE SAD ABSENCE OF DILIGENCE (1:9)

The Apostle now turns the thoughts of the readers in an entirely opposite direction and shows the deplorable effects of a lack of diligence.

1. **Lack of spiritual power:** "He that lacketh these things," *lit.* "He in whom these things are not present." Note the sad picture suggested by these words. The entire absence of all the elements that go to make up a real strong Christian life.

2. **Lack of spiritual perception:** "Is blind, seeing only what is near." Near-sighted Christians are a sad and sorry fact in the Christian Church. This weakness of spiritual sight, insight, and foresight is always due to unfaithfulness in Christian living.

N.B.—Some render the phrase "seeing only what is near," as though it were a transitive verb. "closing the eyes" or "blinking"; suggesting deliberate and wilful action as the outcome of previous unfaithfulness.

3. **Loss of spiritual privilege:** "Forgotten the cleansing from his old sins." The awful possi-

bility here indicated is almost too terrible to contemplate. To think that a man should actually forget the moment and early experiences of his conversion and joy of salvation. Yet all this is clearly regarded as possible, and as resulting from unwillingness to "add diligently" after the reception of God's gifts.

E. THE RENEWED EXHORTATION TO DILIGENCE (1:10)

1. **Its strong incentives:** "Wherefore rather," *i.e.* because of the solemn alternatives just mentioned. The possibilities of failure in Christian life are intended to act as powerful motives to continued and increasing earnestness.

2. **Its personal appeal: "Beloved."** Note the writer's tenderness as he brings these naturally unpalatable truths before the readers. This affectionate appeal is characteristic of the Apostle in his two Epistles (see iii.).

3. **Its definite object:** "To make your calling and election sure." Are these two words synonymous or are they two stages of the Divine process? (cf. Matt. xxii. 14). Note how in 1 Pet. i. 2, 3, the Divine side is mainly emphasized; here it is the human, "make for yourselves." The thought of making our election "sure" suggests the human response of the believer to the Divine revelation. The certitude concerns the believer's own conscious experience of what God's calling and election means.

F. THE PERMANENT OUTCOME
OF DILIGENCE (1:11)

1. **Present steadfastness:** "For if ye do these things ye shall never stumble." Note the strength, the assurance, and the completeness of this promise. Cf. Jude 24, "Able to keep you from stumbling."

2. **Future glory.** The Apostle looks forward as well as around, and encourages his readers with the thought of what diligence will insure to them hereafter.

(*a*) The nature of the glory: "Entrance into the eternal kingdom."

(*b*) The measure of the glory: "Richly supplied." Not a bare entrance, but "sweeping through the gates." Contrast v. 5, R.V., "supply," and v. 11. We supply, and then God will supply. The phrase here has been aptly rendered, "God will spare no expense" as to your entrance into the everlasting kingdom.

THOUGHTS ON THE CHRISTIAN LIFE

1. The Divine provisions (vv. 1-4).
2. The needed earnestness (vv. 5-10).
3. The perfect symmetry (vv. 5-7).
4. The spiritual power (v. 8).
5. The sad possibilities (v. 9).
6. The glorious prospects (vv. 10, 11).

54

CHRISTIAN CERTAINTIES
(2 Peter 1:12-21)

THE exhortations of vv. 5-11 are now confirmed by a personal appeal and by a consideration of the certainties of Christianity as shown by (1) the apostolic witness to Christ, and (2) the prophetic revelation of the Old Testament.

A. PASTORAL SOLICITUDE (1:12-15)

This second section of the Epistle, like the first, commences with a personal reference to the Apostle's relation to his readers.

1. **His personal determination:** v. 12, "Wherefore I will not be negligent." He shows the importance of the truth he is teaching and the great dangers of those to whom he is writing.

2. **His definite purpose:** v. 12, "To put you in remembrance of these things." We see at once in these words his conviction of the importance of truth and his consciousness of their continual need of it.

3. **His gentle reminder:** v. 12, "Though ye know them, and are established in the truth

which is with you." What a characteristic touch is this! He fears to give any impression of complaint or distrust, and so he reminds them that he is doing what might seem to be a work of supererogation. Notice this reference to "establish in the truth." The Greek is "strengthened" (cf. iii. 16, 17; 1 Pet. v. 10; Luke xxii. 32). Peter is thus doing the very work his Master commanded.

4. **His short opportunity** (vv. 13, 14). Evidently he regards his departure as imminent. For "tabernacle" cf. 2 Cor. v. 1-4. The allusion to our Lord's prediction (John xxi. 18) is clear. Peter never forgot that memorable colloquy (1 Pet. v. 2). Note R.V. "swiftly," *i.e.* either "soon," or "swiftly" when it actually comes.

5. **His wise foresight:** v. 15, "After my decease . . . remembrance." For "decease" cf. Luke ix. 31 (Greek), *lit.* "exodus"; a reminiscence of the Transfiguration. What did he mean by making provision for them to remember these things after death? Did he intend to write something more? Or is there a reference to the Gospel of Mark written under his influence? Probably the latter. It is generally thought that the voluminous apocryphal literature of the second century which was issued in the name of Peter was prompted by this verse.

B. PERSONAL TESTIMONY (1:16-18)

The Apostle now strengthens his position by a reference to his own personal witness of the realities of the revelation of Christ. He takes the Transfiguration as the special point of his testimony.

1. **The substance of the message:** v. 16, "The power and coming of our Lord Jesus Christ." Notice the two aspects of the apostolic thought. Some authorities consider that they constitute one phrase, *i.e.* the coming power or powerful coming. Perhaps, however, it is possible to distinguish, and regard the "power" as referring to the first coming of Christ (Rom. i. 4, "with power"), and the "coming" (*lit.* presence) to the second coming of the Lord. It would seem as though the latter word must refer to the second Advent (Jas. v. 7, 8), though Dr. Chase (*Hastings' Bible Dictionary*) thinks the first coming is meant, since the context is historical, not prophetical.

2. **The reality of the message:** v. 16, "Not followed cunningly devised fables." The word translated "fables" is "myths" or allegorical teachings; a favorite word in the Pastoral Epistles (1 Tim. i. 4, iv. 7; 2 Tim iv. 4; Tit. i. 14). The Apostle implies in the words he uses that he had not wasted his time in "tracking carefully out" a lot of "sophistical myths" when he declared to them the Gospel.

3. **The proof of the message:** v. 16, "We became eyewitnesses of His majesty" (Luke ix. 32, 33). The Transfiguration is here regarded as an anticipation of the second coming, "when the Son of man shall come in His glory." In many respects the Transfiguration was a microcosm of

the eternal future. There we see the heavenly glory; the Old Testament saints; the New Testament disciples; the Kingly Son, and the Divine Father.

4. **The corroboration of the message:** v. 17, "He received from the Father honor and glory." The Apostle thus shows that the Father's testimony to His Son was the crowning proof of the power and authority of the Gospel message. Peter's allusion to "the excellent glory" is doubtless a reminiscence of the Shechinah glory of the Transfiguration (Matt. xvii. 5).

5. **The confirmation of the message** (v. 18). Once again the Apostle introduces his own testimony. Not only did he see the glory of the Son, but he heard the voice. (Note St. John's reminiscence of the same event in John i. 14: "We beheld His glory.")

C. PROPHETIC REVELATION (1:19-21)

From apostolic we pass to prophetic testimony to the power and coming of our Lord, just as in 1 Pet. i. 10-12 the Apostle bears his witness to the Divine authority of the Scriptures of the Old Covenant.

1. **The Divine assurance granted:** v. 19, "We have the word of prophecy made more sure." The probable force of this phrase is that Old Testament prophecy had become more sure by being confirmed by the Transfiguration. The coming of Christ was thus the fulfilment of the prophetic testimony. The A.V. can hardly stand here, as it

seems to imply that prophecy is "more sure" than the Divine Voice at the Transfiguration.

2. **The earnest attention required:** v. 19, "To which ye do well that ye take heed." He thus urges upon them a careful study of the Old Testament revelation.

3. **The deep necessity stated:** v. 19, "As a lamp shining in a dark place." This allusion to the "dark place" shows the need of the Divine light about which he is speaking. The word translated "dark" is, literally, "dry," "squalid," and gives the idea of a light showing up the dirt and filth of sin. This was the actual state of the world then (cf. Isa. l. 11; John viii. 12). We see also what Peter thought of prophecy—a light in the midst of squalor. Such is ever the character and power of Scripture.

4. **The glorious expectation described:** v. 19, "Until the day dawn, and the day star arise." This seems to be a reference to the second coming of our Lord. The "day star" first coming as the harbinger of the dawn, and then the glorious appearing following. On this view the words "in your hearts" must be separated from the phrase "until the day star arise," and it would seem best, though it is somewhat awkward, to link "in your hearts" with "take heed," the intervening words being parenthetical. If "in your hearts" is taken with "the day star arise," it implies that the Christians were at that time in darkness, which gives an entirely erroneous idea to the whole meaning of the Apostle.

5. **The definite explanation given** (vv. 20, 21). This is the reason why the Old Testament Scriptures are a light in a dark place. The Apostle tells us that these Scriptures came from God and not from man, and on this account they shed their light over earth's squalid and desert places. The word "interpretation" is found only here in the New Testament, though its corresponding verb is found in Mark iv. 34, "expounded"; Acts xix. 39, "decided," and LXX. of Gen. xli. 12, "interpreted." It means unloosing, unfolding, disclosing. The word "private" is, literally, "its own," and is never rendered "private" in any other passage, though it occurs one hundred and thirteen times. The meaning, therefore, is: no prophecy came of the prophets' own unfolding, for prophecy did not come by the will of man, but by the Holy Ghost. The point of these verses is, in fact, not the *interpretation* of Scripture, but the *origin* of Scripture; not what Scripture *means,* but what Scripture *is.* Any use of the context to oppose "private judgment" is therefore entirely wide of the mark. If, however, it is urged that v. 20 must mean "interpretation," then we must understand an ellipsis in v. 21, "neither can it be interpreted by the will of man"; but there can be little doubt that the former is the true meaning of the passage.

FUTURE NOTES

1. The elements of true ministry

(*a*) Pastoral earnestness (vv. 12, 13, 15).

(*b*) Prominence given to the truth of God (vv. 12, 13, 15, 16, 19, 20, 21).

(*c*) Personal testimony based on personal experience (vv. 16, 18).

Consider how these elements were exemplified in the ministry of Peter, and note the absolute necessity of them in every form of Christian testimony.

2. **The foundations of spiritual assurance.** The Apostle frequently lays stress on "knowledge" as the great safeguard of power and true steadfast Christian living. In the passage before us he states the grounds or foundations of this personal knowledge or assurance.

(*a*) Prophetic revelation (vv. 19-21).

(*b*) Apostolic confirmation (vv. 16-18).

(*c*) Personal attestation (vv. 12, 19).

It will thus be seen that we have here in perfect combination and order the Divine word of truth verified by individual experience. In this combination will be found the absolute guarantee of religious and moral certitude.

55

FALSE TEACHERS (1)
(2 Peter 2:1-9)

THE contrast between i. 19-21 and this chapter is sudden and striking. The one theme is *False Teachers,* and we see the "burning lava of the Apostle's indignation" (Farrar). The whole chapter is virtually one long paragraph, but there are certain stages which mark the course of the thought. We may notice three aspects of these False Teachers and their work.

A. THEIR CHARACTER (2:1)

1. **Illustrated in the Old Testament:** "There arose false teachers also among the people." The force of "also" is to be noted, implying "false" as well as "true" prophets. For Old Testament examples see Deut. xiii. 1-5; 1 Kings xxii.; Jer. xxiii.; Ezek. xiii.

2. **Foretold in the New Testament:** "As among you also there shall be false teachers" (cf. Matt. vii. 15, xxiv. 11f.). These predictions of his Master the Apostle now confirms (cf. Jude 4).

3. **Described by the Apostle.** Three marks of these false teachers are now dwelt upon.

(*a*) They will introduce heresies: "Who shall privily bring in destructive heresies," *i.e.* heresies causing destruction (cf. Phil. iii. 19). Note carefully that "heresy" in the New Testament implies false conduct and not erroneous opinion only. The root idea is that of "choice," indicating deliberate and wilful severance from right thought and righteous paths (cf. Acts xxiv. 5, "sect").

(*b*) They will deny their Lord: "Denying even the Master that bought them." Note these three characteristic words: "deny," "Master," "bought." How striking and significant for Peter to speak of another denial! What memories the word must have called up! (cf. Matt. x. 33). The word for "Master" is our English word "despot," implying absolute lordship and dominion. "That bought them" (cf. 1 Cor. vi. 20, vii. 23; 1 Pet. i. 18, 19). How solemn the thought that these men were doing despite to the Divine purchase of redemption! In the New Testament sense of the word, "heresy" is always a denial of Christ, for it is the determination to go our own way and to set at nought His personal work and authority.

(*c*) They will involve themselves in destruction: "Bringing upon themselves swift destruction" (cf. Phil. iii. 19).

B. THEIR INFLUENCE (2:2-3a)

The following points, describing the effects of the false teachers and their work, bear sad and solemn testimony to the deep-rooted and awful nature of their influence.

1. **It was widespread**: "Many shall follow."

2. **It was immoral**: "Their lascivious doings." A.V. "Pernicious ways" (cf. 1 Pet. iv. 3).

3. **It was blasphemous**: "By reason of whom the way of truth shall be evil spoken of." Christianity as "the Way" is characteristic of the Book of the Acts (Acts ix. 2, xvi. 17, xix. 9, xviii. 25, xxii. 4, xxiv. 14). The phrase "evil spoken of" is, literally, "shall be blasphemed," and it is evident that the sin is tantamount to our modern idea of blasphemy.

4. **It was treacherous**: "And in covetousness shall they with feigned words make merchandise of you." These false teachers were to use "counterfeit" or "fabricated" words in order to deceive their dupes, though all the while their main object was greed of gain and a covetous trafficking in holy things.

C. THEIR DOOM (2:3b-9)

1. **Its certainty stated**: v. 3b, "Whose sentence now from of old lingereth not, and their judgment slumbereth not." The judgment is thus regarded as threatened long ago, but not yet inflicted though absolutely assured. The phrase "lingereth not" is, literally, "is not idle," *i.e.* in working itself out; and the second statement, "slumbereth not," *lit.* "does not blink," is a picturesque assertion of the unerring certainty of punishment.

2. **Its certainty illustrated** (vv. 4-8). Notice here the three examples from the Old Testament to illustrate and confirm the assurance of judgment.

(*a*) By the fall of the angels (v. 4) (cf. Jude 6, see Gen. vi. 1). The Greek describes the place of punishment as *Tartarus—i.e.* the deepest abyss of the lower world. The word is only found here.

(*b*) By the flood (v. 5). Note another allusion to the fewness of those saved at the Flood (1 Pet. iii. 20). See R.V., "Noah with seven others," according to a well-known Greek idom.

(*c*) By the cities of the plain (vv. 6-8). Note the description of Lot as "righteous"; a suggestive and striking comment on and addition to the Old Testament narrative (Gen. xix.). What a picture of personal righteousness in judicial standing with God, combined with sad weakness in spiritual state and condition!

N.B.—The "for if" of v. 4 has no *apodosis* stated. It is evidently implied in the commencement of v. 9.

3. **Its certainty assured** (v. 9).

(*a*) By Divine knowledge: "The Lord knoweth how."

(*b*) By Divine protection of the godly: "To deliver the godly out of temptation."

(*c*) By Divine reservation of the ungodly: "And to keep the unrighteous . . . unto . . . judgment."

SUGGESTIONS

Out of several points arising from this narrative, special attention may be concentrated on the following.

1. **The awful possibilities of evil**
(*a*) Imitating the good.
(*b*) Travestying the good.

(*c*) Destroying the good.

2. **The unerring judgment on sin**

(*a*) Swift (v. 1).

(*b*) Sure (v. 3).

(*c*) Complete (v. 9).

3. **The urgent need of watchfulness**

(*a*) Because error counterfeits good.

(*b*) Because evil lures the good.

(*c*) Because of the intimate connection between error in teaching and evil in practice.

4. **The glorious certainties of the godly**

(*a*) A Divine Redeemer (v. 1).

(*b*) A Way of Truth (v. 2).

(*c*) A Sure Protection (v. 9).

NOTE

As the Greek of this section and of the whole chapter contains a number of unusual words and phrases, it has been thought best to give a general idea of the main thought without entering upon a detailed comment of words and phrases. For a due consideration of these, one of the leading Greek Commentaries, like Alford and Bigg, is essential.

56

FALSE TEACHERS (2)
(2 Peter 2:10-22)

A FURTHER and fuller description of False Teachers especially those of the worst sort (v. 10). The passage is difficult to follow in full detail. St. Jude should be read closely side by side with this. Note that the evil is regarded as existing among those who had made profession of Christianity. The treatment seems to follow the same general line as in vv. 1-9, dealing with character, influence, and judgment.

A. CHARACTER DESCRIBED (2:10-16)

1. **Licentiousness:** v. 10, "Chiefly them that walk ... defilement." Note again this reference to uncleanness as a mark of these false teachers. "Lust of defilement" means "a lust that hankers after pollution."

2. **Wilfulness:** vv. 10, 11, "Despise dominion . . . rail at dignities." Who are the "dignities" whom these false teachers despise? Some think angels, though it is difficult to see how this can be. Probably it refers to wilful contempt of all authority, especially that of our Lord. Verse 11

is obscure and difficult. Perhaps the best interpretation is of good angels. When withstanding evil, angels do not abuse their opponents— how much more should evil men avoid doing so! "The angels standing "before the Lord" never forget the dread of that Presence" (cf. Jude 9).

3. **Brutishness:** v. 12, "Creatures without reason, born mere animals." Another reference to self-indulgence.

4. **Recklessness:** v. 12, "Railing in matters whereof they are ignorant," *lit.* blasphemy.

5. **Sensuality:** v. 13, "Count it pleasure to revel in the daytime." Riotousness in daytime was regarded as the acme of self-indulgence and sin (Acts ii. 15; Rom. xiii. 13; 1 Thess. v. 7).

6. **Hypocrisy:** v. 13, "Spots . . . feast with you" (cf. R.V.). A difference of reading here. The idea seems to be that these false and evil teachers associated themselves with the Christian love-feasts, and yet all the while were living in sin.

7. **Infamy:** vv. 14-16, "Cannot cease . . . enticing." Here we sound the depth of their sin. Not only do they themselves indulge in awful iniquity, but actually entice weak and young Christians in the same direction. Note the reference to Balaam, and see Num. xxxi. 8, 16 for the point of its appropriateness.

B. INFLUENCE DEPICTED (2:17-19)

1. **Emptiness:** v. 17, "Springs without water." No real vitality.

2. **Instability:** v. 17, "Mists driven by a storm." No settled principles or position.

3. **Boastfulness:** v. 18, "Great swelling words of vanity." Bluster in order to dupe."

4. **Seductiveness:** v. 18, "They entice . . . lasciviousness." Another reference to the awful character of their life.

5. **Heartlessness:** v. 18, "Those who are just escaped." Note this appeal to passions in dealing with unsettled souls just converted (cf. Matt. xviii. 6).

6. **Deception:** v. 19, "Promising them their liberty." A striking temptation to the newly converted.

7. **Powerlessness:** v. 19, "They themselves are bondservants." The real character of the men.

C. DOOM DECLARED (2:20-22)

We now have brought before us in vivid and solemn detail the outcome of this false teaching in terrible judgment on those who practiced it.

1. **Sinful entanglement:** v. 20, "Entangled therein." This is the first stage. They are in the meshes of the net which, however, is not yet closed upon them.

2. **Moral disaster:** v. 20, "And overcome." This follows as the result of the entanglement to those who are unwilling to break through the net.

3. **Spiritual degeneration:** v. 20, "Last state is become worse" (cf. Matt. xii. 43-45). A clear allusion to the Master's teaching.

4. **Utter apostasy:** vv. 21, 22, "Turning . . . wallowing." The Apostle says it were better that they had not known the way of righteousness, because the Gospel had been tried unfairly and the fault and sin of the failure was theirs (cf. Heb. vi. 4-6, x. 26). Note the terse description of Christianity here as the "holy commandment" (cf. 1 Tim. vi. 14). Christianity is thus summed up in a word implying holiness and obedience, character and conduct. Mark the word "delivered" (v. 21, cf. Jude 3). For v. 22 see Prov. xxvi. 11. Contrast the sow returning to the mire, and the sheep returning to the shepherd (1 Pet. ii. 25). The merely reformed character often returns to his sin, but the saved sinner, who backslides, returns to the Shepherd of souls.

5. **Merited punishment:** vv. 12, 13, "Destroyed . . . shall receive the reward." "Wronging, they shall be wronged." The A.V. of v. 13, "receive the reward of unrighteousness," seems to be intended as sarcastic.

6. **Divine condemnation:** v. 14, "Children of cursing" (see similar phrase Eph. ii. 3; 2 Thess, ii. 3; 1 Pet. i. 14). They shall receive the curse of Divine judgment upon sin.

7. **Everlasting ruin:** v. 17, "Blackness of darkness . . . for ever."

N.B.—It seems best to regard these particulars of judgment as applicable to the false teachers rather than to the young converts whom they lead astray. If the allusions in vv. 20-22 are to recent converts, the description of hopelessness and ruin seems almost incredible. In the case of teachers who have done such despite to truth and purity as is seen in vv. 10-19, such a description of utter ruin is entirely appropriate.

GENERAL THOUGHTS

In the course of this terrible passage, many truths are brought to our notice. Among them we may specify.

1. The awful possibilities of sin

(*a*) The prevalent character: sensuality and coveteousness.

(*b*) The association of sin with religion.

(*c*) The deliberate opposition to truth.

2. The terrible nature of apostasy

(*a*) Light without life (cf. Heb. vi. 4, "enlightened").

(*b*) Profession without possession.

(*c*) Sin without compunction.

3. The adequate safeguards of discipleship

(*a*) "The way of truth" (v. 2); "the way of right" (v. 15); "the way of righteousness" (v. 21).

(*b*) "The knowledge of the Lord and Saviour" (v. 20).

(*c*) "The holy commandment" (v. 21).

NOTE

The note subjoined to the last study is, if possible, still more applicable to this in view of the many new and strange Greek words and phrases.

57

SAFEGUARDS
(2 Peter 3:1-10)

THE third section opens with another personal reference to his purpose in writing and the need of the reminder in view of the prevalence of scoffers. Note how he describes the special point of the scoffing and then answers it.

A. THE EARNEST CALL (3:1-2)

1. **Its affectionate tone:** v. 1, "Beloved." Four times in the chapter this word occurs, showing clearly the Apostle's tender and humble tone as contrasted with the Apostolic authority which he might have used.

2. **Its practical purpose:** v. 1, "To stir up your sincere mind . . . remembrance." Thus he resumes i. 12, 13, wishing "thoroughly to arouse" them, though it is so soon ("now") since he wrote his first letter. He bears hearty testimony to the reality of their spiritual life by speaking of their "sincere mind" (or thought) (Phil. i. 10; 1 Cor. v. 8; 2 Cor. i. 12, ii. 17). This is in marked contrast with the darkened minds of the false teachers of ii. (cf. Eph. iv. 18).

3. **Its special appeal:** v. 2, "That ye should remember the words . . . and the commandment." As in i. 16-21, the Apostle here unites a reference to Old Testament prophecy and apostolic teaching, and desires to concentrate their attention on this teaching with all its special application to the dangers surrounding them. Note the singular number of "commandment" as summing up apostolic teaching (cf. ii. 21).

B. THE URGENT MOTIVE (3:3-4)

The Apostle now explains why he makes this earnest appeal. It is because of the dangers ahead, which may be described as threefold.

1. **Scoffing:** v. 3, "Mockers shall come." Mark the phrase, "knowing this first," as in i. 20, indicating special attention. The "last days" seem to refer to the close of the Messianic dispensation (cf. Isa. ii. 2; Acts ii. 17; Heb. i. 2; Jas. v. 3; 1 Pet. i. 20). Scoffing has not been limited to any one age of the Church. See Ps. i. 1.

2. **Sinfulness:** v. 3 "Walking after their own lusts." The connection of scoffing with evil living is noteworthy; the latter is almost invariably an accompaniment of the former.

3. **Scepticism:** v. 4, "Where is the promise?" *i.e.* "the fulfilment of the promise" (cf. Isa. v. 19). This is the doctrinal error which underlay the sinful life of the false teachers. The "fathers" seem to refer to Old Testament times (Rom. ix. 5; Heb. i. 1).

C. THE THOROUGH EXPOSURE
(3:5-7)

The Apostle proceeds to show the unreality and deliberate sin of the attitude just described.

1. **Wilfulness revealed:** v. 5, "This they wilfully forget." We can thus see the true meaning of the scoffing and sin. It is due solely and entirely to deliberate wilfulness. "Evil is wrought for want of *will*" to do good.

2. **Wilfulness corrected:** vv. 5, 6, "The world . . . perished." He shows that the assumption of immutability made by the scoffers is unwarranted and untrue. The world had not always been unchanged, for the flood had taken place; water was always there, ready to do God's will. See R.V. of this verse and Gen. i. 6-10.

3. **Wilfulness warned** (v. 7). The scoffers are told that as formerly water was God's instrument, so now fire is available, and only waiting for God's time. Note the emphasis on "reserved" (R.V. "stored up," ii. 4-9; 1 Pet. i. 4).

N.B.—It has been suggested that we have in this chapter a reference to three distinct heavens: (1) the heavens that were of old (v. 5); (2) the heavens that now are (v. 7); (3) the new heavens (v. 13). On this interpretation v. 6 will refer to some catastrophe which happened between the events recorded in Gen. i. 1, Gen. i. 2, thus producing the chaos mentioned in Gen. i. 2 as "without form and void; but it seems best to interpret v. 6 of the flood. The scoffers are thus solemnly warned that though God may delay, His judgments are certain and His instrument ready at hand.

D. THE COMPLETE EXPLANATION
(3:8-10)

Now for the sake of the Christians who may possibly be themselves perplexed by the delay, a clear statement is given of the facts of the case. The explanation is found in the character and purpose of God.

1. **The perfect wisdom of God:** v. 8, "One day . . . as a thousand years" (cf. Ps. xc. 4). The difference between the Divine and human computation of time is here clearly shown as one part of the explanation of apparent delay.

2. **The longsuffering mercy of God:** v. 9, "Not wishing" (cf. Ezek. xviii. 23, xxxiii. 11). Thus these scoffers were actually rejecting God's mercy and doing despite to His longsuffering which extended even to them if they would but see it.

3. **The absolute righteousness of God:** v. 10, "The day of the Lord will come." Thus the longsuffering is balanced by the justice, and we are told of—

(*a*) The certainty of the coming: "Will come."

(*b*) The character of the coming: "As a thief" (cf. Matt. xxiv. 43; Luke xii. 39; 1 Thess. v. 2; Rev. iii. 3, xvi. 15).

(*c*) The consequences of the coming: "In the which the heavens . . . the elements . . . the earth." It will then be clearly seen that nature is far from immutable. Note these references to physical convulsions as accompanying the day of God (cf. Mark xiii. 24; Isa. xxxiv. 4; li. 6). The "elements" seem to be the heavenly bodies in this verse.

SUGGESTIONS

1. Some elements of unbelief
(*a*) Doctrinal error (v. 5).
(*b*) Contemptuous opinion (v. 4).
(*c*) Impure conduct (v. 3).
Note the order of these three elements, and how the outward expression is stated first by the Apostle (v. 3), and the trouble then traced to its source.

2. Some encouragements to faith
(*a*) The word of God remembered (v. 2).
(*b*) The wisdom of God trusted (v. 8).
(*c*) The warning of God heeded (vv. 9, 10).

58

LAST WORDS
(2 Peter 3:11-18)

THE Epistle draws to a close with some personal and practical exhortations based on the foregoing warnings and instructions.

A. THE BELIEVER'S HOPE

1. Its substance

(*a*) "The day of the Lord" (v. 10).

(*b*) "The day of God" (v. 12).

Is it possible that these two expressions mark two stages of the future? "The day of the Lord" is to come as a thief, and to be associated with physical catastrophes. "The day of God" is spoken of as that time *on account of which* (Greek) these physical convulsions are to take place, and as ushering in "the new heavens and the new earth." The day of the Lord, from its first mention in Isa. ii. 12, is always associated with terror and judgment. Possibly we may distinguish, and say that the day of the Lord represents our Lord's coming to judgment before the millennium (Rev. xx), while the day of

God is the ushering in of Eternity, when God shall be "all in all" (1 Cor. xv. 28). In any case the Christian's hope is set on "the crowning day that is coming."

2. Its accompaniments

(*a*) The dissolution of the present order (v. 11).

(*b*) The introduction of a new order (v. 13).

Thus an exact analogy will take place in the future through fire as took place in the past through water (Gen. ix. 11). See Isa. lxv. 17, lxvi. 22; Rev. xxi. 1.

3. Its character (v. 13)

(*a*) It is to be righteous: "Righteousness."

(*b*) It is to be permanent: "Dwelleth," *i.e.* where righteousness has its fixed abode. This will be the remarkable contrast to the present state of things, wherein seems to dwell so much unrighteousness.

4. **Its warrant:** v. 13, "According to His promise" (cf. vv. 4, 5). This is the foundation of Christian hope, the sure word of God (i. 19; Acts iii. 21).

B. THE BELIEVER'S ATTITUDE

The Apostle now enlarges very fully on the various and varied aspects of the Christian life and conduct in view of the glories and solemnities of the future.

1. **Expectation** (vv. 12-14). Note the emphasis on "looking," *lit.* "expecting."

2. Earnestness

(*a*) In service: v. 12, "Earnestly desiring," or "hastening" (see R.V. and R.V. marg.). The A.V.

"hasting unto" is not accurate. It must mean either "earnestly longing for" or "hastening." It implies eagerness for the coming, and that eagerness shown in prayer ("Thy kingdom come") and effort. Who knows whether the coming has not been delayed by reason of the unfaithfulness of Christians?

(*b*) In character: v. 14, "Give diligence." Not only in relation to others, but in relation to our own life the Apostle urges earnestness.

3. Holiness

(*a*) Of conduct: v. 11, "What manner . . . in all holy living and godliness?" The plurals of the original (Greek) are expressed in the italic "all" of A.V. and R.V. The verse is very strong. "What sort of persons it is necessary for you to continue to be in all kinds of holy behavior." For "behavior" cf. I Pet. i. 15, a favorite word of the Apostle.

(*b*) In character: v. 14, "In peace, without spot and blameless in His sight." Contrast the spots and blemishes of the false teachers in ii. 13. In these two phrases, "spotless" and "unblemished," we see the character God intends us to possess.

4. Reverence: v. 11, "All forms of . . . godliness." Another instance of a word almost entirely associated with St. Peter and St. Paul, implying the attitude of godly fear.

5. Assurance: v. 14, "Found of Him in peace." This describes the attitude of the believer as he meets his Lord without shame (1 John ii. 28, iv. 17).

6. Patience: v. 15, "Account that the long-suffering of our Lord is salvation," *i.e.* it gives time

for salvation. This thought is intended to stimulate the readers to endurance of present problems and opposition (cf. Rom. ii. 4; ix. 22).

7. **Watchfulness:** v. 17, "Seeing ye know, beware lest ye . . . fall." Forewarned is forearmed, as the Apostle clearly shows.

8. **Growth:** v. 18, "But grow" (cf. i. 2, 8). Thus grace opens and closes this Epistle. It is clearly implied that they are already in the grace, and they are to grow and make progress therein.

9. **Praise:** v. 18, "To Him be the glory." In spite of the perplexities and defections and oppositions the Christians are exhorted to praise God. "Both now and unto the day of eternity." The latter phrase is found only here.

C. THE BELIEVER'S SECRET

The Christian's attitude in view of the hope that is set before him is only made possible by a careful consideration and personal realization of the secrets and conditions of holiness and progress laid down in the Word of God. Of these conditions there are four named or suggested in this passage.

1. **Divine teaching** (vv. 15, 16). The allusions in these verses to the Scriptures, both of the Old and New Testament, clearly indicate the necessity and value of God's revelation for growth in the Christian life, and for the maintenance of the believer's true attitude whether in opposition to the dangers around or in reference to the glories of the future.

N.B.—The reference to Paul is given as a confirmation of this call to patience. It tells its own story of (1) the true and brotherly relations between Peter and Paul; (2) the estimate already given to the Epistles of Paul, which are thus associated with the Old Testament Scriptures as the Word of God. Ignorant and unsteadfast souls were already "twisting" Paul's writings. Probably the reference is a general one, or it may be specifically to his Epistles to the Galatians, Ephesians, and Colossians, included in the Churches of Asia Minor, to which St. Peter was writing (1 Pet. i. 1). It is thought with great probability that it was St. Paul's doctrine of Justification which was particularly in view as "wrested unto their own destruction." For "unstable" cf. i. 12, ii. 14; 1 Pet. v. 10. It is significant and important to notice that though Scripture difficulties and misconceptions are mentioned, the Scriptures themselves were not on this account withheld from the people.

2. **Divine warning:** v. 17, "Beware lest . . ." The Christians are here clearly reminded in affectionate terms ("beloved") of the dangers besetting them, and of the possibility of their own failure in face of them. The Apostle is anxious lest they should "fall once for all" (see Greek).

3. **Divine grace:** v. 18, "In grace." Their position as ensphered by grace is here brought to their notice. Grace surrounds and upholds, grace is the atmosphere of their life, and as they abide in it they are to "keep on growing" (Greek). It

is only by continuous growth that the possibility of a terrible fall is effectually prevented.

4. **Divine fellowship:** v. 18, "Knowledge of our Lord and Saviour." This also is part of the sphere and atmosphere of their spiritual existence. Knowledge of God here, as elsewhere, always implies personal experience and conscious fellowship, and in this is one of the prime secrets of Christian steadfastness and progress. Thus the Epistle ends as it began, with its keynote of "knowledge."

59

GLEANINGS (1)

In the study of the life and writings of the Apostle Peter a large number of subsidiary topics arise out of the main narratives and discussions. Some of these, mainly word-studies, may now be suggested in barest outline as an incentive to further discoveries. There are few more profitable methods of Bible study than a consideration of the particular topics which suggest themselves in the course of the study of any book or section.

1. Grace

1. Grace multiplied (1 Pet. i. 2; 2 Pet. i. 2).
2. Grace coming (1 Pet. i. 10, 13).
3. Grace of life (1 Pet. iii. 7).
4. Manifold grace (1 Pet. iv. 10).
5. Grace to the humble (1 Pet. v. 5).
6. God of grace (1 Pet. v. 10).
7. True grace (1 Pet. v. 12).
8. Grow in grace (2 Pet. iii. 18).

2. Precious Things

1. The trial of faith (1 Pet. i. 7).
2. The blood of Christ (1 Pet. i. 19).

3. The grace of the Lord Jesus (1 Pet. ii. 7, R.V.).
4. Spiritual character (1 Pet. iii. 4).
5. Faith (2 Pet. i. 1).
6. The promises (2 Pet. i. 4).

3. Brother-Love

1. As a purpose of redemption (1 Pet. i. 22).
2. As a proof of submission (1 Pet. ii. 17).
3. As an indication of reality (1 Pet. iii. 8, iv. 8, 9).
4. As an encouragement of faith (1 Pet. v. 9).
5. As an element of character (2 Pet. i. 7).

4. Diligence

1. In relation to strong faith (2 Pet. i. 5).
2. In relation to sure calling (2 Pet. i. 10).
3. In relation to earnest service (2 Pet. i. 15, Greek).
4. In relation to future glory (2 Pet. iii. 12, Greek and iii. 14).

5. Well-doing

1. Eliciting praise (1 Pet. ii. 14).
2. Silencing evil (1 Pet. ii. 15).
3. Involving suffering (1 Pet. ii. 20).
4. Imitating example (1 Pet. iii. 6).
5. Causing persecution (1 Pet. iii. 17).
6. Guaranteeing protection (1 Pet. iv. 19).
7. Heeding Scripture (2 Pet. i. 19).

6. Behaviour

This word **(anastrophe and cognates)** means "conduct," not speech. Mark its characteristics.

296 / The Apostle Peter

1. Holy (1 Pet. i. 15; 2 Pet. ii. 11).
2. Reverent (1 Pet. i. 17).
3. Vain (1 Pet. i. 18).
4. Beautiful (1 Pet. ii. 12, Greek).
5. Domestic (1 Pet. iii. 1).
6. Pure (1 Pet. iii. 2).
7. Good (1 Pet. iii. 16).
8. Unclean (2 Pet. ii. 7).
9. Erroneous (2 Pet. ii. 18).

7. Fear

Godly reverence is very marked in 1 Peter, a significant thought in view of his former character.
1. Fear shown in conduct (1 Pet. i. 17).
2. Fear of God (1 Pet. ii. 17).
3. Fear in subjection (1 Pet. ii. 18).
4. Fear in chaste behaviour (1 Pet. iii. 2).
5. False fear (1 Pet. iii. 6, 14).
6. Fear with courage and meekness (1 Pet. iii. 15).

8. Glory

1. At Christ's appearing (1 Pet. i. 7).
2. The reward of sufferings (1 Pet. i. 11).
3. Associated with rejoicing (1 Pet. iv. 13).
4. Personal participation (1 Pet. v. 1).
5. Its crown (1 Pet. v. 4).
6. The Divine purpose (1 Pet. v. 10).

9. Steadfastness

See the Greek word here (*sterizein*).
1. The Master's command (Luke xxii. 32).
2. The Divine assurance (1 Pet. v. 10).

3. The blessed secret (2 Pet. i. 12).
4. The terrible contrast (unsteadfastness, 2 Pet. ii. 14, iii. 16).
5. The solemn possibility (2 Pet. iii. 17).

10. Hope

1. Its character (1 Pet. i. 3).
2. Its endurance (1 Pet. i. 13, R.V.).
3. Its object (1 Pet. i. 21, iii. 5).
4. Its possession (1 Pet. iii. 15).

11. Called

1. To holiness (1 Pet. i. 15).
2. To light (1 Pet. ii. 9).
3. To suffering (1 Pet. ii. 21).
4. To blessing (1 Pet. iii. 9).
5. To glory (1 Pet. v. 10).
6. By Divine power (2 Pet. i. 3, R.V.).

12. The Apostle's Expectation

1. Everlasting inheritance (1 Pet. i. 4).
2. Salvation (1 Pet. i. 5, 9).
3. Praise and glory (1 Pet. i. 7).
4. Grace (1 Pet. i. 13).
5. Glory (1 Pet. iv. 13, v. 10).
6. Judgment (1 Pet. iv. 17).
7. Reward (1 Pet. v. 4).
8. The Chief Shepherd (1 Pet. v. 4).
9. Everlasting kingdom (2 Pet. i. 11).
10. The day of the Lord (2 Pet. iii. 10).
11. The day of God (2 Pet. iii. 12).
12. New heavens and earth (2 Pet. iii. 13).

60

GLEANINGS (2)

13. Peter's Three Sleeps

1. The sleep of unripe experience (Luke ix. 32).
2. The sleep of unfaithful life (Mark xiv. 37).
3. The sleep of unquestioning trust (Acts xii. 6).

14. Incorruptible Things

1. Incorruptible inheritance (1 Pet. i. 4).
2. Incorruptible ransom (1 Pet. i. 18).
3. Incorruptible seed (1 Pet. i. 23).
4. Incorruptible character (1 Pet. iii. 4).

15. Abundance

1. Grace and peace multiplied (1 Pet. i. 1; 2 Pet. i. 1).
2. Christian life (2 Pet. i. 8).
3. Everlasting glory (2 Pet. i. 11).

16. Suffering

1. Of Christ (1 Pet. i. 11, ii. 23, iii. 18, iv. 1, 13, v. 1).
2. Like Christ (1 Pet. ii. 21, v. 1, 9).
3. For Christ (1 Pet. ii. 19-21, iii. 14, 17, iv. 15, 19, v. 10).

17. Beautiful Things

The Greek word *kalos* means goodness which is outwardly attractive.
1. Beautiful behavior (1 Pet. ii. 12).
2. Beautiful works (1 Pet. ii. 12).
3. Beautiful stewards (1 Pet. iv. 10).

18. Reserved

1. Heaven for the godly (1 Pet. i. 4).
2. Hell for the ungodly (2 Pet. ii. 4, 9, iii. 7).

19. Knowledge

1. Knowledge of God in Christ (2 Pet. i. 2, 3, 8, ii. 20, iii. 18).
2. Knowledge of the way of righteousness (2 Pet. ii. 21).
3. Knowledge in Christian character (2 Pet. i. 5, 6).

20. Ready

1. Salvation to be revealed (1 Pet. i. 5).
2. Defence to be offered (1 Pet. iii. 15).
3. Judgment to be declared (1 Pet. iv. 5).

21. Virtue

The New Testament use seems to mean either "energy" or "excellence."
1. Referring to God (1 Pet. ii. 9; 2 Pet. i. 3, R.V.).
2. Referring to Christians (2 Pet. i. 5: cf. Phil. iv. 8; 1 Pet. ii. 9, "show forth *the virtues of Him*").

22. Unspeakable Things

1. Unspeakable joy (1 Pet. i. 8).
2. Unspeakable words (2 Cor. xii. 4).
3. Unspeakable gift (2 Cor. ix. 15).

23. God spared not

1. The angels (2 Pet. ii. 4).
2. The antediluvian world (2 Pet. ii. 5).
3. His Son (Rom. viii. 32).

24. Exultation

1. In view of future glory (1 Pet. i. 6).
2. In view of present grace (1 Pet. i. 8, iv. 13).

25. Without Spot and Blemish

1. Christ had none (1 Pet. i. 19).
2. Christians should have none (2 Pet. iii. 14).
3. Non-Christians do have them (2 Pet. ii. 13).

26. Knowing this first

1. The Divine origin of Scripture (2 Pet. i. 20).
2. The human contempt of truth (2 Pet. iii. 3).

27. Manifold

1. Trials (1 Pet. i. 6).
2. Grace (1 Pet. iv. 10).

28. Death

1. Divestiture (2 Pet. i. 14).
2. Departure (2 Pet. i. 15).
3. Entrance (2 Pet. i. 11).

29. Manifestation

1. Christ's first coming (1 Pet. i. 20).
2. Christ's second coming (1 Pet. v. 4).

30. *Hyparhein* (Permanence)

This word implies a continuous and permanent state of being, and thus understood has great point in these passages.

1. Permanent possession of graces (2 Pet. i. 8).

2. Permanent possession of corruption (2 Pet. ii. 19).

3. Permanent character expected (2 Pet. iii. 11).

31. Salvation

1. Present (1 Pet. iii. 21; 2 Pet. iii. 15).

2. Future (1 Pet. i. 5, 9, 10, ii. 2, R.V., iv. 18).

BIBLIOGRAPHY

LIFE AND CHARACTER OF THE APOSTLE PETER

Alexander: *Expositor,* Third Series, Vol. IV. pp. 184, 266.
Bartlett: *Century Bible*—Acts.
Birks: *Studies in the Life and Character of St. Peter.*
*Bruce: *The Training of the Twelve.*
Chase: *Hastings' Bible Dictionary,* article on Simon Peter.
Hackett: *Commentary on the Acts of the Apostles.*
Howson: *Horae Petrinae.*
McGarvey: *New Commentary on Acts.*
Parker: *The People's Bible*—Acts.
Robinson: *Simon Peter—his Life and Times.*
Seeley: *The Life and Writings of St. Peter.*
Stifler: *An Introduction to the Book of the Acts.*

*Published by Kregel Publications, Grand Rapids, Michigan

Taylor: *Peter the Apostle.*
Thomas: *Homiletic Commentary on the Acts of the Apostles.*
Thompson: *Life-work of Peter the Apostle.*

THE EPISTLES OF ST. PETER

Alford's *Greek Testament.*
Balfour on 1 Pet. iii. 18-20: *Expository Times,* Vol. VII p. 356.
Bennett: *Century Bible—* 1 & 2 Peter.
Bigg: *International Critical Commentary—*1 & 2 Peter.
Brown: *Expository Discourses on First Peter.*
Bullinger: *Figures of Speech used in the Bible.*
Caffin: *Pulpit Commentary—*1 & 2 Peter.
Chase: *Hastings' Bible Dictionary* on 1 & 2 Peter.
Cook: *Speaker's Commentary—*1 Peter.
Hort: *The First Epistle of St. Peter,* i. 1—ii. 17.
Johnstone: *Commentary of the First Epistle of Peter.*
Kelly: *The First Epistle of Peter.*
Leighton: *Commentary on 1 Peter.*
Lillie: *Lectures on the Epistles of Peter.*
Lumby: *Speaker's Commentary—*2 Peter; *Expositor's Bible—*The Epistle of St. Peter.
Lumby: *Expositor,* First Series, Vol. III. p. 264, Vol. IV. pp. 113, 448.
Masterman: *The First Epistle of St. Peter.*
Thornley Smith: *Lectures on the First and Second Epistles of Peter.*
Welch and others on 1 Pet. iii. 18-20: *Thinker,* Vol. VI. pp. 129, 144, 337, 420, 527.
Weymouth on 1 Pet. iv. 6: *Thinker,* Vol. VIII. p. 33.
Withrow on 1 Pet. iii. 18-20: *Homiletic Review,* Vol. XX. p. 403.
Withrow on 1 Pet. iv. 6: *Homiletic Review,* Vol. XXI. p. 319.

*Published by Kregel Publications, Grand Rapids, Michigan

SCRIPTURE INDEX